LITURGICAL EVANGELISM

LITURGICAL EVANGELISM

Robert E. Webber

MOREHOUSE PUBLISHING
Harrisburg, PA

Morehouse Publishing

Editorial Office
871 Ethan Allen Highway
Ridgefield, CT 06877

Corporate Office
P.O. Box 1321
Harrisburg, PA 17105

Library of Congress Cataloging-in-Publication Data
Webber, Robert.
    [Celebrating our faith]
    Liturgical evangelism / Robert E. Webber.
        p.   cm.
    Originally published: Celebrating our faith. San Francisco :
Harper & Row, 1986
      ISBN 0-8192-1596-1 (paper)
      1. Evangelistic work.   2. Initiation rites—Religious aspects—Christianity.
3. Public worship.
[BV3793.W39   1992]   92-22224
265'.13—dc20   CIP

Printed in the United States of America
by
BSC Litho
Harrisburg, PA 17105

Contents

7. The Rite of Initiation   84

   The converting process culminates in the rite of initiation. Baptism
   symbolizes the forgiveness of sin, chrismation represents admittance
   into the people of God, and receiving the Eucharist symbolizes sharing in the life of the Holy Spirit.

8. Mystagogia   99

   During this period of postbaptismal instruction, the newly born
   spiritual infant is integrated into the life of the church.

Epilogue   109

Bibliography   113

Index   115

Preface

Over the past decade, the evangelism of unbelievers and the restoration of baptized but lapsed people has become a primary concern of almost every major denomination. Some denominations are returning to mass evangelism, while others are turning toward one-on-one evangelism. Behind all the attempts to revive evangelism lies the universally expressed longing to restore an evangelism that belongs to the local church. Christian leaders want an evangelism that not only converts people, but also brings them into the full life of the church and keeps them there.

This book focuses on local church evangelism. It does not propose a new gimmick or the creation of one of America's fastest growing churches. This book advocates restoring third-century evangelism, an evangelism that was used effectively in the context of a secular and pagan society.

This form of evangelism has also been revived in the Catholic church today by decree of the councils of Vatican II. For more than a decade, the Catholic church around the world has been successfully experimenting with the adaptation of this third-century form of evangelism, which I have called *liturgical evangelism.*

This evangelism is thoroughly evangelical and catholic. It is evangelical because it is rooted in the historical gospel of Jesus. It is catholic because it was developed out of biblical precedent by the universal church. Its roots can be traced back to the New Testament and its development can be followed through the second century into its full flowering in the third century. While liturgical evangelism continued in the fourth and fifth century, it became dissipated by the priority given to infant baptism over adult baptism and the alleged Christianization of the Roman Empire.

The modern Catholic version of this ancient evangelism is called the *rite of Christian initiation of adults* (RCIA). It is still in its experimental stage and thus subject to adaptation not only in Catholic congregations, but also in Protestant churches as well.

In this book I wish to introduce liturgical evangelism to the Protestant church. I firmly believe liturgical evangelism is readily adaptable to all Protestant denominations. It is also rapidly becoming the evangelism par excellence of the local church. Consequently, I have made my presentation of the subject simple and straightforward. Except for the opening chapter, each chapter presents the biblical background, the experience of the early church, and the contemporary application of the tradition through liturgical evangelism.

I also want to provide a sourcebook for the people of a local church—pastors, laypersons, members of decision-making bodies—who intend to implement liturgical evangelism within their own congregation. For this reason the book is characterized by a pastoral dimension. While it is not a how-to book, its content is arranged in such a way that any local church desiring to implement liturgical evangelism could do so by following the steps discussed in each chapter.

I have many people to thank. Primarily, I wish to acknowledge the authors of the books cited in the text. They have done much of the spade work by gathering historical and contemporary information on the RCIA.

1. What Is Liturgical Evangelism?

Liturgical evangelism calls a person into Christ and the church through a conversion regulated and ordered by worship. These services order the inner experience of repentance from sin, faith in Christ, conversion of life, and entrance into the Christian community.

St. Mark's Episcopal Church in downtown Philadelphia is an old stone church squeezed in among a row of refurbished colonial homes and shops. There, in 1978, I went on a mission that was destined to affect me more than it did the people of St. Mark's. My task was to speak on evangelism in a Friday evening service, then conduct a workshop on the subject the following Saturday morning.

What the congregation expected or even wanted from me was not clear. I only knew St. Mark's was a church interested in reaching its neighborhood with the gospel. In preparation for the workshop, I considered various methods of evangelism recorded in Scripture. I found myself returning to an idea born of a conversation with an evangelical leader. I had given this person a gift of *The Book of Common Prayer.* After reading through the liturgies of the church, he came to me and declared, "Why, there is more gospel in the liturgy than you will find in a typical evangelical church in a month of Sundays."

No one will dispute that the liturgies of the church, whether Catholic, Orthodox, Anglican, Lutheran, or other denomination are filled with the gospel. The gospel is present in the prayers, the Scripture readings, the Apostles' Creed, the kiss of peace, and supremely in the Eucharist. At the table of the Lord, the gospel is not only verbalized, but also dramatized in the physical symbol of the Eucharist.

My theme at St. Mark's Episcopal Church, which was "The Gospel in the Liturgy," developed this idea. "Here in your hands," I declared, "you hold the greatest gift for evangelism and renewal available to your church." I elaborated on this theme by showing how the weekly celebration of the liturgy proclaims and reenacts the death and resurrection of Jesus Christ for the renewal of the world. I called this liturgical evangelism.

My experience at St. Mark's helped me to put into focus the basic principle of liturgical evangelism: worship is a means through which we may evangelize people into Christ and his church. At the time I was unaware that this principle, which is an ancient principle of the church, was being revived and reinstated by the contemporary Catholic church. However, the principle developed by the Catholic church was broader in scope, perhaps even more basic than what I presented at St. Mark's. Treating worship as a key to evangelism, the contemporary Catholic church has revived a local church method of evangelism that was used effectively in the second- and third-century church.

A chief source for our knowledge of evangelism in the early church is *The Apostolic Tradition* written around 215 A.D. by Hippolytus, a bishop in Rome. In this document Hippolytus reveals the method and content of evangelism in the early church. The method was a process, not a one-time decision made under emotional pressure without a support community. This process brought a person into Christ and full communion with the Christian community through the periods of development and growth related to baptism. For example, the following stages of conversion can be discerned in *The Apostolic Tradition:* (1) a period of inquiry, (2) a time of instruction, (3) an intense spiritual preparation for baptism, and (4) continued nurture in the church. Further, each of these periods is set off by a passage rite that marks the transition to the next period of growth. These passage rites include (1) the rite of entrance into the time of instruction, (2) the rite of election into the intense period of spiritual preparation, and (3) the rites that surround baptism. Consequently, we may discern four periods of growth and development framed by three rites of passage. These seven parts constitute the framework of liturgical evangelism.

Within this sevenfold process, four basic principles of liturgical evangelism can be discerned: (1) Christ as victor over the powers of evil, (2) the church as a nurturing and mothering community, (3) the power of external rites to order internal experience, and (4) the principle of growth into Christ and the church through various stages of development. This chapter comments on each of these principles and thus clarifies the meaning of liturgical evangelism more fully.

CHRIST AS VICTOR OVER THE POWERS OF EVIL

According to Gustaf Aulen, the fundamental view of Christ's work held by the early church is *Christus victor.* [1] This theme, which may be traced back to the Pauline writings, perceives the world in terms of a conflict between light and darkness, Christ and Satan, the kingdom of God and the kingdom of evil. This biblical story begins with creation and the fall and extends into the future to the end of history. The scope of the story is cosmic and includes everything from creation to re-creation. The elements of the story, such as the fall, the covenants, the incarnation, the death, burial, and resurrection, the ascension, and Pentecost, as well as the history of the church and its anticipation of the future, tell of Christ's conquest over evil.

The Christian makes the confession of faith that Christ is victor over sin, death, and the dominion of the devil. He has "disarmed the principalities and powers and made a public example of them, triumphing over them" (Col. 2:15). Yet the victory of Christ over the powers of evil is no mere intellectual proposition. It is essentially a doxological affirmation, a proclamation of praise, a liturgical affirmation. Thus, in worship the church experiences this victory and cries "Jesus is Lord" (Rom. 10:9), "Hallelujah! For the Lord our God the Almighty reigns" (Rev. 19:6). The church joins heavenly worship in its hymn to Christ the victor, "To Him who sits upon the throne and to the Lamb be blessing and honor and glory and might forever and ever!" (Rev. 5:13).[2]

Through liturgical evangelism a person is brought into an experience of Christ as victor. In this process the converting person is turned away from following the "prince of the power of the air" and is made "alive together with Christ" (Eph. 2:1–10). In the early church, this process of conversion was ordered around the rites that culminated in baptism and entrance into the Christian community. Through these rites the new Christian experienced Christ as Lord over the powers of evil.

This emphasis on the experience of Christ's present lordship over the powers of evil is clearly evident in the rite of initiation. It is expressed, for example, in the exorcisms, the renunciation of evil by the baptismal candidate, the anointing with the oil of thanksgiving, and the eucharistic prayer. The words of the eucharistic prayer represent a climax in the process of conversion and coalesce the entire experience of turning away from sin toward Christ, the victor over the powers of evil.

A unique feature of the baptismal journey and the culminating eucharistic experience is that *my* story and *his* story converge. The Christ story is the overarching story that gives meaning to my story through the incorporation of my story into his. This one story, is captured in the biblical image of Christ as the second Adam (Rom. 5:12–21). We are all related to the first Adam, who, because of his sin, brought us under the dominion of death and condemnation. Were it not for the second Adam, Christ, we would all be left in the state of condemnation and alienation from God. The second Adam is the hero who brings righteousness, life, and justification. Only through Christ can the human condition and that of the entire universe be restored and renewed. Consequently, the baptismal journey makes one a participant in the story set forth in the eucharistic prayer. This story, for which we give thanks, locates Christ in a cosmic setting. He who is one with the Father became incarnate in the womb of the Virgin Mary, destroyed death by his death, tread down hell by his resurrection, and gained for himself a holy people, the church.

The liturgy of the church celebrates this true story through reenactment. Through baptism one makes the journey to union with Christ who, by his destruction of the powers of evil, makes fellowship with God in the earthly life of the church possible. The Eucharist repeatedly celebrates the victory of Christ over the powers of evil, a celebration that brings the healing effect of the Christ event to the worshiping community again and again.

This supernatural conception of Christ as victor over the powers of evil and thus Lord of the cosmos and Lord and Savior of my life lies at the heart of liturgical evangelism. The evangelism of the early church did not seek to evangelize people into a cosmic idea, a myth, or a mere window to the Father. For the early church, Jesus was the incarnate Son of God, victor over sin, Savior of those who repented and put their faith and trust in him as Lord.

THE CHURCH AS A NURTURING AND MOTHERING COMMUNITY

A second principle of liturgical evangelism in the early church asserts that conversion into Christ takes place through the church. The church, far from being a mere aggregate of human persons, is, from the standpoint of evangelism, the mother in whose womb God's children are born, the mother who offers her breast for nurture and sustenance.

The theme of *Ecclesia Mater* originates in both the Old and New Testament and is rooted in the fusion of the symbols of bride and groom.[3] For example, the relationship between God and Israel is depicted in Isaiah, chapters 61–62, and Jeremiah, chapters, 25, 33, as that between a bride and bridegroom. This marriage relationship between God and Israel is expressed in the mystical union between Christ and the church in the New Testament (Eph. 5:21–33). Consequently, at the end of history, the holy city, the new Jerusalem that is understood as the church, is proclaimed to be the bride of the Lamb (Rev. 21:9).

The early church fathers drew on the image of the bride to develop the feminine and mothering qualities of the church. Perceiving a mystical union between Christ and the church, they stressed the need to be converted to Christ in and through the church. Cyprian declared that "he can no longer have God for his father who, has not the church for his mother."[4]

Descriptions of the church as mother abound among the

early church fathers. Tertullian speaks of "Our Lady Mother the Church" who nourishes us "from her bountiful breasts."[5] Clement of Alexandria extols the church as "Virgin and Mother—pure as a virgin, loving as a mother."[6] Cyprian, whose writings on the church are replete with female imagery, proclaims the church to be "the one mother copious in the results of her fruitfulness. . . . by her womb we are born, by her milk we are nourished, by her spirit we are animated."[7]

But how does the church fulfill its mothering role? First, according to the early church fathers, the church is the womb in which God's children are born. This image of gestation appears as early as the second century in the *First Apology* of Justin Martyr, a work written to the Emperor Titus to explain the Christian faith. Justin describes the church as a womb and draws an analogy between the water of baptism and the "moist seed" of conception. In the water of the church, the candidate is washed "in the name of God the Father and Lord of the universe, and of our Saviour Jesus Christ, and of the Holy Spirit." For Christ said, [6]"Except ye be born again ye shall not enter into the Kingdom of Heaven.' "[8] In the womb of the church, conversion to Christ is conceived. And the water of baptism, which is the unique possession of the church, symbolically represents the creation of new life.[9]

Second, the church is mother because of the quality of the nurture it provides. Augustine is so assured of the loving nurture of the church that he can say, "You are safe who have God for your Father and His Church for your Mother."[10] In his treatise on baptism, Augustine stressed both the birthing and nurturing aspects of the church. The church "gives birth to all . . . within her pale, of her own womb."[11] The church brings to birth, nurses, cares for, and even agonizes over her children. In spite of these statements, Augustine acknowledges that not all who are in the church are of God. Some may stray from the naming that was done over the waters. These repudiate their birthright and disclaim God's ownership of their lives. Those "who are born within the family, of the womb of the mother herself, and then neglect the grace they have received, are like Isaac's son Esau, who was rejected, God Himself bearing witness to it, and saying, 'I loved Jacob, and I hated Esau; and that though they were twin-brethren, the offspring of the same womb.' "[12]

Liturgical evangelism, then, is evangelism in and through the church. It is not mass evangelism, para-church evangelism, or even one-on-one evangelism. While each of these models of evangelism may feed into liturgical evangelism, liturgical evangelism takes place in the context of the local church, of the mystery of faith that is experienced and modeled by a local spiritual family born and nurtured by its mother, the church.[13]

THE POWER OF EXTERNAL RITES TO ORDER INNER EXPERIENCE

Another principle of liturgical evangelism in the early church recognizes that external rites have the power to order an inner experience. This principle, which unites external action and internal reality, is rooted in the Christian doctrine of incarnation. The confession that the human and divine are united in the person of Christ affirms that God can and does work through material and physical creation. The rites of initiation make God and his saving presence a reality through physical signs. In order to clarify this principle, I have set forth eight statements that will illuminate more clearly the idea that external rites order inner experience.[14]

First, the rites of initiation must be seen as commemorating an historical event. The historical reference point for liturgical evangelism is the life, death, and resurrection of Jesus Christ. In the Christian vision of reality, this story rises above all other stories of life. We may be enchanted by the stories of Abraham or the life of Moses, the glorious account of a David or a Paul, but these stories, important as they may be in the Christian family, cannot compare with the story of Christ set forth in the Gospels. As Christians our ultimate identity is found not with Moses, David, or Paul, but with Jesus Christ. Liturgical evangelism, then, particularly in the rites of initiation, connects our story, our life, and our journey with the one story, the one person from whom and through whom our life gains ultimate meaning.[15] By this means our inner experience of living, dying, and being resurrected with Christ is ordered and accomplished.

Second, the external process of liturgical evangelism symbolically represents the original Christ event. Liturgy, like art, seeks to bring us into the truth. For example, the very form of the rite of initiation—its design, its symbols, its sequence, its content—illuminates the original event of Christ. It represents what is fundamental, what is enduring and essential, what is central to the gospel in its action of representing the truth. Consequently, this evocative form lifts the original event from its historical roots and brings it down through the corridors of time into the present moment.

Third, the sevenfold process of liturgical evangelism is the external agency through which the belief of the Christian community is handed down to the new believer. All forms of evangelism require an external agent that will break in upon the recipient, distress that recipient with a sense of sin, and arouse that person to faith. Faith results from the work of the Holy Spirit, which sometimes acts through the agency of personal witness and at other times acts through proclamation. However, in the case of liturgical evangelism, the Holy Spirit incites contrition and faith by the entire process of initiation. These stages of conversion and passage rites symbolically organize, assist, and carry along the inner experience of the soul. Thus, the process itself—what is symbolized —and the sequence through which it proceeds represent the faith of the community and present God's call to faith, awaiting the soul's desire.

Fourth, liturgical evangelism may next be seen as a way of ordering and giving shape to Christian experience. It is not a series of events that the participant judges. One does not set oneself against the periods of formation, for that would be presumptuous. Rather, the person places himself or herself under the process of initiation and freely allows it to name the experience of conversion. When the recipient feels the process speaking in his or her heart and realizes an inner correspondence to the meaning that the outer forms symbolize, that person is truly named as Christ's own and led into a deeper relationship with God.

Fifth, the symbolic forms employed in liturgical evangelism cannot be exhausted intellectually. The rites of liturgical evangelism, such as the inquiry, the catechetical period, the exorcisms, the washing with water, anointing with oil, and so on, are all prelogical forms of expression. These ritual forms of communication cannot be exhausted by logical inquiry or empirical investigation. These symbols communicate through the senses to a level of consciousness that lies deeper than our thoughts. The point of contact in human personality that builds the bridge between this world and the next is not the mind, but the heart.

Sixth, liturgical evangelism, to function in the ways described previously, has a sacramental character and ought not to be regarded as merely illustrative. If the process of initiation only illustrates and informs, we cannot speak of the rites as embodying the original event they represent. Unlike illustration, sacrament is participatory. It is incarnational, commingling the physical and the spiritual. Thus, through the rites the conversion that is represented may actually take place. The rites must be seen as a necessary element of the process, for they not only represent the Christ event, but they also embody the event, so that the participant actually enters into the Christ event and its saving reality through the participatory experience of the rites observed.

Seventh, because liturgical evangelism is sacramental, it requires faith. Faith, of course, is not in the thing itself but in that which it embodies, namely, Jesus Christ. In liturgical evangelism the person also carries a responsibility to discern truth, to exercise his or her will to affirm and intend what is represented.

Finally, then, the response of faith to the event represented in the rite creates participation in the reality the rite represents. Participation in Christ and his church is the goal of evangelism. Evangelism that only brings a person to a detached intellectual acquiescence is not evangelism at all. It is a mental affirmation of God who exists as the other alongside of the self. Evangelism strives to accomplish not a mere recognition of God, not a mere acknowledgement of his existence, but a participation in the life of Christ through the life of the church in which he dwells. This inwardness is achieved not by the rejection of the external rites and orders of the church, but by the recognition that these rites, attended by the desire of the soul, actually bring us into participation, into relationship with Christ and the salvation he brings.

The actual ordering of the rite of initiation, together with the symbolic gestures that signify the meaning of the action taking place, give shape to and order the inner experience of conversion—but not without the faith and intention of the convert.

GROWTH IN CHRIST THROUGH VARIOUS PERIODS OF DEVELOPMENT

A final principle of liturgical evangelism in the early church recognizes that growth into Christ and the church is subject to process and development. This assertion does not preclude the possibility of instant conversion. Certainly, there have been and will always be conversions "on the road to Damascus." But even these conversions require development and nurture that may be represented by stages of maturation and growth. For example, St. Paul went away to Arabia, then, after three years, went to Jerusalem for fifteen days to confer with Cephas. Next, he went off to the regions of Syria and Cilicia. And finally, fourteen years after his conversion, he went to Jerusalem and on to his famous missionary work (Gal. 1:15–2:1). Exegetes agree that these fourteen years were a time of growth and development for Paul. Like Jesus, who "increased in wisdom and in stature, and in favor with God and man" (Luke 2:52), Paul underwent periods of growth and maturation. Consequently, liturgical evangelism looks upon conversion into Christ and the church as a process that, even if preceded by a dramatic conversion, still requires a person to develop over time a responsible and dynamic relationship with Christ and the church.

The notion of process and development was not foreign to the early church fathers. Irenaeus, for example, refers to growth this way: "Man has first to come into being, then to progress, and by progressing come to manhood, and having reached manhood to increase, and thus increasing to persevere, and by persevering be glorified, and thus see his Lord."[16] Even more interesting, Irenaeus argues that Christ himself sanctified the various stages of human life. "He came to save all through his own person; all, that is, who through him are re-born to God; infants, children, boys, young men and old. Therefore he passed through every stage of life."[17] Today, the insights of Jean Piaget's cognitive developmental structuralism, Erik Erikson's psychosocial theory, and James Fowler's stages of spiritual growth provide a fertile contemporary basis for the restoration of an evangelism that takes into account various periods of development.[18]

The process of conversion consists of a series of readily identifiable stages of development. The period of *inquiry* presupposes an interest in the gospel; next, the *catechumenate* presupposes a certain degree of commitment; the period of *intense spiritual preparation* before baptism assumes a resolute determination and an inner resolve to identify with Christ; the *rite of initiation* (baptism) is a turning point, a crisis moment in which one plunges fully into a relationship with Christ; this results in the final period, that of *incorporation into the church*, participation in the body of Christ, and an acceptance of responsibilities implied by belonging to the family of faith.

In this chapter I have defined liturgical evangelism as a *conversion experience regulated and ordered by the liturgical rites of the church*. This evangelism presupposes that Christ is victor over sin, insists that the church plays a mothering role in conversion, regards external rites as a means through which an inner experience of faith is ordered, and allows that conversion into Christ and the church occurs through various periods of faith and development.

Now, more than when I first spoke at St. Mark's Episcopal Church in Philadelphia, I am persuaded that worship is a major context for evangelism. At that time I was not fully aware of the approach to evangelism in the early church. This book intends to place in a contemporary context this ancient form of evangelism for churches like St. Mark's. The early church practiced a form of evangelism that brought the whole community of faith into the process of conversion and renewal. It promised to renew not only the lives of individuals, but also the life of the whole church. It had the potential to assist an entire community not only to experience anew the mystery of God's love in Jesus Christ, but also to be formed into the body of Christ.

NOTES

1. Gustaf Aulén, *Christus Victor* (New York: Macmillan, 1969).
2. For the development of the *Christus victor* theme as related to the powers of evil, see Hendrik Berkhof, *Christ and the Powers* (Scottsdale, Pa.: Herald Press, 1977); Clinton D. Morrison, *The Powers That Be* (Naperville, Il.: Alec R. Allenson, Inc., 1960); G. B. Caird, *Principalities and Powers* (London: Oxford University Press, 1956); Heinrich Schlier, *Principalities and Powers in the New Testament* (New York: Heider & Heider, 1961); John Howard Yoder, *The Politics of Jesus* (Grand Rapids, Mich.: Eerdmans, 1972).
3. For this and other images of the church, see Paul S. Minear, *Images of the Church in the New Testament* (Philadelphia: The Westminster Press, 1960).
4. Cyprian, *On the Unity of the Catholic Church*, 6. Quoted from the *Ante-Nicene Fathers*, compiled by A. Cleveland Coxe (Grand Rapids, Mich.: Eerdmans, 1971) vol. V, 423. hereafter referred to as ANF.
5. Tertullian, *On Martyrdom*, 1. ANF, vol. III, 693.
6. Clement, *The Instructor*, Bk. I, 6. ANF, vol. II, 220.
7. Cyprian, *Unity of the Church*, 5. ANF, vol V, 423.
8. Justin Martyr, *First Apology*, 61. ANF, vol. I, 183.
9. An excellent expansion of this whole theme is found in Tertullian, *On Baptism*. ANF, vol. III, 669–679.
10. Augustine, *Against Petilian*, bk. III, 9–10. *The Nicene and Post-Nicene Fathers* (Grand Rapids, Mich.: Eerdmans, 1957) vol IV, 601. Hereafter referred to as PNF. Edited by Philip Schaff.
11. Augustine, *Against Donatists*, bk. I, 15–23. PNF, vol. IV, 421.
12. Ibid, 14.
13. For further development of the theme of church as mother among the early

church fathers, see Michel Dujarier, "A Survey of the History of the Catechumenate," in *Becoming a Catholic Christian,* ed. William J. Reedy (New York: Sadlier, 1981), 19ff.

14. For an extended argument on the incarnational principle that external rites shape internal experience, see Adrian Nichols, O.P., *The Art of God Incarnate: Theology and Symbolism from Genesis to the Twentieth Century* (New York: Paulist Press, 1980).

15. For further development of the gospels as story, see John Shea, *Stories of God: An Unauthorized Biography* (Chicago: Thomas More Press, 1978) and James B. Wiggins, ed., *Religion as Story* (New York: Harper & Row, 1975).

16. Irenaeus, *Against Heresies,* bk. IV, 38, 2–3, in *The Early Christian Fathers* translated by Henry Bettenson (Oxford: Oxford University Press, 1969), 68.

17. Ibid, bk. II, 22, 4. Bettenson, 80.

18. See Jean Piaget, *Structuralism,* trans. C. Maschler (New York: Basic Books, 1970); Erik Erikson, *Childhood and Society* (New York: Norton, 1950); James Fowler, *Stages of Faith: The Psychology of Human Development and the Quest for Meaning* (San Francisco: Harper & Row, 1981).

2. Inquiry

The period of inquiry opens the door of the church to the person who has heard the gospel and wishes to pursue it more fully.

My father was the pastor of the Montgomeryville Baptist Church, a church located about twenty-five miles west of Philadelphia. It is an old church, dating back to the 1700s; tradition had it that George Washington once worshiped there. Whether the legend is true or not, it is indeed an old church surrounded by a large cemetery with tombstones of Indians and many other people dating as far back as the early seventeenth century.

My own preevangelism began when, as an adolescent, I read the epitaphs of people who left an enduring testimony inscribed on a roughly hewn tombstone in the cemetery. I suspect that I always believed the faith, having grown up in an atmosphere of belief in God and trust in Christ. But my spiritual sensibilities were jarred, even more fully awakened, when I was thirteen. My father said, "Robert, don't you think it's time you became baptized?" For reasons that I could not then give, the image of baptism forced me to inquire more deeply into myself to determine whether or not my intentions of faith were strong enough to allow for a step as decisive as entrance into the waters of baptism. My father's question forced me to personalize the gospel, to acknowledge I was a sinner in need of the saving grace of Jesus Christ, to recognize I was part of the fallen creation in need of a new birth. In other words, *Christ's* question created my inquiry.

This illustrates the meaning of the period of inquiry. It is a time to awaken faith, a time to receive Christ, a time to set one's face in the direction of baptism. Consequently, during inquiry the claim of Christ is presented, the gospel is preached, and the invitation to accept Jesus as Lord and Savior is made.

THE BIBLICAL ROOTS

Although the New Testament does not use the term *inquiry*, the concept is everywhere assumed. Inquiry simply asserts that conversion into Christ presupposes an initial encounter with truth. For example, the model for this encounter is found in Christ himself. He began his ministry by insisting that "the time is fulfilled, and the Kingdom of God is at hand; repent, and believe the gospel" (Mark 1:15). He called people into decision: "You cannot serve God and mammon" (Matt. 6:24). He demanded, "If you would be perfect, go, sell what you possess and give to the poor, and you will have treasure in heaven; and come, follow me" (Matt. 19:21). These radical statements as well as others like them were designed to confront the hearer with truth, to create interest in the gospel, and to clarify what it means to follow after Christ.

The model of encounter with truth was also used in the primitive Christian community. On the day of Pentecost, Peter proclaimed the life, death, and resurrection of Christ and concluded his sermon with the words, "Let all the house of Israel therefore know assuredly that God has made him both Lord and Christ—this Jesus whom you crucified" (Acts 2:36). Luke described the result: "When they heard this they were cut to the heart" (Acts 2:37). The message had hit home, it penetrated into their hearts and created inquiry: "Brethren, what shall we do?" To which Peter responded, "Repent and be baptized every one of you in the name of Jesus Christ for the forgiveness of your sins." (Acts 2:37–

38). The inquiry "Brethren, what shall we do?" was the beginning of a journey, a journey that would lead into baptism and finally into full incorporation into the church, and into the body of Christ.

This sense of journey, a movement from one phase of spiritual awareness to another, provides us with insight into the content of preevangelism in the primitive community. The Pentecost narrative in Acts seems to imply a twofold movement for the inquirer (Acts 2:14–36). The first step proclaims the mystery of the gospel and awakens faith, cutting the listeners "to the heart" and prompting them to ask "what shall we do?" When the listeners come to faith, they are invited to take the second step—to repent and be baptized "in the name of Jesus Christ for the forgiveness of your sins; and you shall receive the gift of the Holy Spirit." (Acts 2:38)

This twofold sequence is also illustrated by Paul in his letter to the Thessalonians. Here, in one of the earliest books of the New Testament, Paul speaks of the Thessalonian journey in faith as a movement away from former ties to new commitments of faith. "You turned to God from idols" (1 Thess. 1:9). This twofold sequence is repeated throughout the book of Acts, suggesting a basic pattern or movement into Christ that was common to other communities of faith (see Acts 16:30; Acts 22:8–10; and Luke 3:10). These narratives suggest that in the primitive Christian community, adults were not baptized into the church unless they demonstrated faith in Jesus Christ by turning away from their former commitments.

The inquiry in the New Testament era was based on a preaching of the gospel that called upon people to believe in Jesus, to turn away from their pagan way of life and take up the new life. Both beliefs and practices were taught from the gospel in greater depth during the catechumenate. Inquiry, which may have been initiated by preaching, personal witness, or the life of a living apostle, was more informal than formal. It summoned believers to faith, invited them to enter into the journey of the faithful, and appealed to them to become a member of a new society, the household of faith. Those who were initially persuaded of the truth of Christianity entered into a process that was to lead into a full conversion, baptism, and entrance into the church. We cannot assume that all who entered this process remained through baptism nor that all who were baptized stayed in the church (2 Tim. 4:10).

Consequently, we may regard evangelism as more than the initial proclamation of the church. It consisted of the larger process whereby a person was brought into the church through several phases that deepened and strengthened faith. The first phase was the inquiry, which consisted of the proclamation of Christ as Lord and the call to repent, to turn from their pagan ways to the new life in Christ.

THE EXPERIENCE OF THE EARLY CHURCH

Michael Green, in his classic *Evangelism in the Early Church,* [1] provides us with insight into the evangelistic methods of those first several centuries of the church. The methods of evangelism did not differ from those employed in the New Testament period. These consisted of preaching in formal and informal situations, personal testimony to neighbors and friends, home evangelism, which extended beyond members of the family to both slaves and freed men, and literary evangelism through popular and more academic works.[2]

Evangelism in the early church was always an evangelism

into faith in Christ and a new way of life. It was not enough simply to awaken faith. To be evangelized meant to be brought into a family, into the household of faith, into a community of people who lived differently. This primitive community of faith saw reality in a different way.

Evangelism in the early church must be put into the context of the paganism of the Roman Empire. The people of the Roman world were steeped in an immoral way of life. They believed in many gods, relied on magic, and had faith in the stars. Consequently, evangelism had to confront them on two levels: belief and way of life. Conversion required time to wean them away from their former pagan way of life and teach them the life of faith in Christ. For this reason the early church developed a more formal approach to the inquiry, the initial stage of this twofold task, than what appears in the pages of the New Testament.

Imagine for a moment that you are a new convert from a life of immorality, belief in magic, and a commitment to the emperor as a kind of god. Assume that you have responded in faith to the proclamation of the gospel as a result of the example and witness of a neighbor. What now? As part of the inquiry, you will be brought before the leaders of the local church, who, through discussion with you, will determine how serious you are about the faith and will also tell you briefly what kind of belief and way of life is expected from members of the Christian community.

Fortunately, the details of this part of the inquiry have been summarized for us by Hippolytus in *The Apostolic Tradition:*

Those who come forward for the first time to hear the word shall first be brought to the teachers [at the hours] before all the people come in. And let them be examined as to the reason why they have come forward [to the faith]. And those who bring them shall bear witness for them whether they are able to hear. Let their life and manner of living be enquired into, [whether he has a wife and] whether he is a slave or free. If he be the slave of a believer and his master permit him, let him hear. If his master does not bear witness to him, let him be rejected. If his master be a heathen let him be taught "to please his master" that there be no scandal. If a man have a wife or a woman a husband, let them be taught the man to be contented with his wife and the woman to be contented with her husband. A man who is unmarried let him be taught not to commit fornication but either to marry lawfully or to abide (steadfast). But if there be one who has a devil, let him not hear the word from the teacher until he be cleansed.

[They shall enquire about the crafts and occupations of those who are brought for instruction]. If a man be a pander who supports harlots either let him desist or let him be rejected. If a man be a sculptor or a painter, he shall be taught not to make idols. If he will not desist, let him be rejected. If a man be an actor or one who makes shows in the theatre, either let him desist or let him be rejected. If a man teach children worldly knowledge, it is indeed well if he desist. But if he has no other trade by which to live, let him have forgiveness. A charioteer likewise [or one who takes part in the games or who goes to the games], either let him desist or let him be rejected. A man who is a gladiator or a trainer of gladiators or a huntsman (in the arena) or one concerned with wild-beast shows or a public official who is concerned with gladiatorial shows, either let him desist or let him be rejected. If a man be a priest of idols or a keeper of idols, either let him desist or let him be rejected. A soldier who is in authority must be told not to execute men; if he should be ordered to do it, he shall not do it. He must be told not to take the military oath. If he will not agree, let him be rejected. A military governor or a magistrate of a city who wears the purple, either let him desist or let him be rejected. If a catechumen or a baptised Christian wishes to become a soldier, let him be cast out. For he has despised God. A harlot or a sodomite [or one who has castrated himself] or one who does things which may not be spoken of, let them be rejected for they are defiled. A magician shall not even be brought for consideration. A charmer or an astrologer or an interpreter of dreams or a mountebank [or a clipper of fringes of clothes] or a maker of amulets, let them desist or let them be rejected. If a man's concubine be [a] slave, let her hear [on condition that] she have reared her children, and if she consorts with him alone. But if not let her be rejected. If a man have a concubine let him desist and marry legally; and if he will not, let him be rejected. [And if a baptised woman consort with a slave, either let her desist or let her be rejected.]

[If we have omitted anything, decide ye as is fit; for we all have the Spirit of God.][5]

What interests us here is not only the existence of the inquiry, but also its content. What did the church say to someone who had tasted of the goodness of the Lord and now wanted to pursue the faith deliberately and with intention? No one answers this question more clearly than Hippolytus. But we must keep in mind that the inquiry as set forth by Hippolytus already represents a step beyond the initial hearing of the gospel. We can assume that the person who has come to the leaders of the church has already responded favorably to the initial proclamation of the gospel through a neighbor or friend or through one or another means of hearing the gospel.

Consequently, the purpose of the inquiry held by the leaders of the church is both to proclaim Christ and to expound on what it means to take up the cross and follow after him. The spirit of the inquiry is to show those who "once followed the course of this world" what it means to become a child of God (Eph. 2:1–10). This is not a Salvation by works, but a work that flows from faith. This test weeds out the uncommitted and charts a path for the committed.

The inquiry emphasizes a commitment to a new way of life, even if that means changing vocations. A vocation related in any way to the powers of evil, such as that of a maker of idols, a heathen priest, or an enchanter, must be given up. Any occupation or way of life that leads one into immorality, such as pandering, licentiousness, or keeping a concubine, must be rejected. Anyone in an occupation that leads to killing, such as a gladiator or anyone connected with gladiatorial exhibitions, a soldier, or a civil magistrate who has power over the lives of others, must desist or be rejected. Those who come to the church for the wrong reason will not remain. And those who have begun a genuine conversion will commit themselves to the next phase of the journey.

The inquiry implies that Christianity is more than a belief system, it is a way of life. The inquiry emphasizes saying no to the kingdom of evil that has been overcome by the power of Christ, exhibited in his death and resurrection. Baptism is an identification with Christ's victory over sin. Those who are to be baptized into his death must learn to "walk in newness of life" (Rom. 6:4). Baptism signifies that "our old self was crucified with him so that the sinful body might be destroyed, and we might no longer be enslaved to sin" (Rom. 6:7). Christian life is rooted in *Christus victor.* Someone who claims to follow Jesus and becomes baptized yet lives in darkness according to the course of this world is no better than Simon Magus (see Acts 8:9-24), whose soul, according to Cyril of Jerusalem, "was not buried with Christ, nor raised with him."[4]

The inquiry also implies that external commitments have the power to shape an internal experience. In the third century, it was not enough to have a subjective experience of faith. Faith was to result in works: "Faith apart from works is dead" (James 2:26). Far from being a salvation by works, the inquiry recognized that a commitment to a Christian life has the effect of producing faith. Such a behavioral modification produces an inner experience by means of the external habit. But it does not work without intention, as is clear in the case of Simon Magus and those who come to the inquiry without intention and fall away. For the convert must intend to adopt the way of life in all its manifestations, turning away from darkness and following Christ the light. This is not an instant accomplishment done in the secret chambers of the heart, but, as the inquiry suggests, a life-long public commitment, a process that begins with responding in faith to the gospel of Jesus Christ, repenting from an old way of life, and entering a new life.[5]

APPLICATION TO THE CONTEMPORARY CHURCH

Now the question must be asked: Is the inquiry that was prominent and visible in the church of antiquity useful to the church today, and if so, how?

First, it must be remembered that the cultural context in which the inquiry originally flourished was pagan. The church's power was antithetical to the powers that ruled the state and the society during the first three centuries of its existence. Today the church also exists in many pagan contexts. In China, and other countries where the government takes an avowed atheistic stand, a commitment to a Christian world view and way of life takes on a meaning that stands in greater antithesis to society than it does in Western countries characterized by a veneer of Christianity. Behind the iron curtain, a price is exacted from those who are in the church. Reports confirm that the price is higher for those whose journey has taken them more deeply into the church. For them, it is one thing to attend church, it is another to be baptized, and still another step to commune at the table of the Lord regularly. Each step distances the iron curtain Christian from an attachment to earthly powers, for with each step the relationship with Christ and the church becomes more intense. Many third world countries are also steeped in a pagan context. The population is often given to superstitious and magical views of reality.

In the Western world, despite the increasing pressure of secularization, a radical commitment to Christ is more feasible, though it still runs counter to cultural norms. While it is acceptable to be superficially Christian in the Western world, it is not particularly acceptable to be deeply committed to a way of life that reflects the gospel.

In each of the three cultural situations just described, the church that seeks to be more than a mere institution or social club will recognize the pagan nature of its surrounding culture and will seek to become God's alternative community. By adopting the ancient church's methods, the church in its time of inquiry will be able to clarify the gospel and determine the intent of the inquirer.

Second, the assumption that the inquiry is a viable element of evangelism today presupposes a congregation with a commitment to evangelism. There is a vicious cycle here; many Christians are not involved in evangelism because the local church neither encourages it nor has an effective process for dealing with the new convert. An effective evangelism must simultaneously encourage Christian people to share their story of faith with neighbor and friend and create the inquiry as a formal way of dealing with people who are genuinely interested in converting to Christ. Active church members will be more likely to do initial evangelism if there is a support community in the church to carry converts through the various stages of conversion. To bring a person who shows interest in the gospel into a church that has no ordered means of organizing and deepening his or her experience with Christ is self-defeating.

Third, Christian congregations that wish to nourish new converts in the faith will need to become a community of faith that actualizes the mothering role of the church. In general most Western congregations are a collection of individuals who *go* to church rather than a community of people who *are* the church. This perverts the meaning of church that was experienced in the early communities of faith and advocated by the reformers. John Calvin, for example, echoed the church fathers' concept of the church as mother. "There is no other way to enter into life unless this mother conceive us in her womb, give us birth, nourish us at her breast, and lastly, unless she keep us under her care and guidance until, putting off mortal flesh, we become like the angels (Matt. 22:30). Our weakness does not allow us to be dismissed from her school until we have been pupils all our lives. Furthermore, away from her bosom one cannot hope for any forgiveness of sins or any salvation."[6]

Happily, Catholic and Protestant leaders today share a desire to restore the church to a community in which faith is experienced rather than to perpetuate it as an institution where people gather. In *Paul's Idea of Community,* Robert Banks expresses this desire. "The gospel is not a purely personal matter. It has a social dimension. It is a communal affair. To embrace the gospel, then, is to enter into community."[7]

But the spiritual purpose of this community far outweighs the social element in importance. The community of faith is a realized event of Christ's presence. It is thus the context in which Christ meets with and is met by his people. In worship, prayer, song, Scripture, Eucharist, and sharing, the family life of God's people molds, shapes, supports, and directs the ongoing evangelism and nourishment of the entire community. Avery Dulles, in *Models of the Church,* rightly speaks of this model as the central theme of the early church. Its goal is "to lead men [and women] into communion with the divine" for "whenever men [and women] are in the church they have partly fulfilled the aim of their existence; they are, at least inchoatively, in union with God."[8]

Fourth, the assumption that conversion takes place in stages necessitates an inquiry, for it acknowledges that external rites order internal experience. The alternative is a congregation that does not evangelize or a congregation that assumes all conversions result in an instant transformation of worldview and way of life that permits the convert immediate and full access to the whole life of the community and requires from that convert signs of instant maturity.

Many Protestant churches repudiate a sacramental view of conversion that recognizes the validity of external aids to internal development. The liberals who have thrown away a supernatural view of the gospel have created churches that at worst are social clubs and at best institutions that exist for the promotion of humanitarianism. Evangelicals who believe in the supernatural actually practice a kind of sacramental approach to conversion that recognizes the power of the external rite. The call to raise the hand, stand, walk the aisle, kneel in prayer, confess, and then believe, followed by the admonition to read your Bible, pray, witness, and attend the church of your choice, is an abbreviated external process that mirrors the internal experience. People with either a catholic sacramental conscience or an evangelical decisional process will most readily be attracted to the ancient form of liturgical evangelism and the inquiry. The inquiry helps the inquirer personalize faith in Christ—a purpose both sacramental and decisional.

Finally, a church that does set up the inquiry as a primary period within evangelism must be certain that the persons in charge are able to model conversion. In the ancient church, this was the role of the sponsor. In the modern church, the term *sponsor* is still used among Catholics and is being revived according to its original intent.

Evangelicals practice discipleship by putting a new Christian under the tutelage of a more mature Christian. In liturgical circles this person is known as a spiritual director. Regardless of the term used, the function is still the same. Gregory Michael Smith discusses the role of the mentor (another term) in a very important and helpful book, *The Fire in Their Eyes: Spiritual Mentors for the Christian Life.* "One element seems consistent with peoples' discovery of new religious potential. That single constant factor is best described as the presence of a facilitating person. Such a person can act as a spiritual mentor or guide. This person assists and encourages growth by being a kind of life reference, a person who senses and draws out the greatness that lies beneath—hidden and untapped."[9] At the time of inquiry, a converting person may be given a mentor who, during the journey into the church, can function as (1) an advocate of growth, (2) a listener, (3) a prayer partner, (4) a reconciler of issues and (5) a witness to the new life.[10]

The first period of the spiritual journey into Christ and the church[11] begins with the hearing of the gospel, a hearing that is clarified and affirmed by the local church in the inquiry. We have seen the inquiry in its developed form in the early third century, we have traced its roots back to the New Testament, and we have urged the establishment of a process of conversion in the local church today that begins with the inquiry and moves through distinct phases of development toward baptism and full incorporation into the church.

A local congregation should strive to achieve an evangelism that falls upon good soil and springs up a hundredfold. This is best accomplished when the seeds are watered, the weeds are pulled out, and the sun shines sufficiently and without scorching. In inquiry the tender shoot is cultivated and nurtured so that the shoot will grow into a blooming plant.

NOTES

1. Michael Green, *Evangelism In the Early Church* (Grand Rapids, MI: Eerdmans, 1970).

2. Ibid., chap. 8.

3. For the text see *The Treatise on the Apostolic Tradition of St. Hippolytus of Rome,* ed. Gregory Dix and Henry Chadwick (Harrisburg, PA: Morehouse Publishing, 1992), 23-28.

4. Cyril of Jerusalem, *Protocatechesis.* prologue, 2 *The Nicene and Post-Nicene Fathers.* vol. VII, ed. Edwin Hamilton Gifford (Grand Rapids, MI: Eerdmans, 1974), 1.

5. See E. Glenn Hinson, *The Evangelization of the Roman Empire* (Macon, Ga.: Mercer University Press, 1981), 74–95.

6. John Calvin, *Institutes of the Christian Religion.* ed. John McNeil, bk. 4 (Philadelphia: The Westminster Press, 1960), 4.

7. Robert Banks, *Paul's Idea of Community* (Grand Rapids, MI: Eerdmans, 1980), 33.

8. Avery Dulles, *Models of the Church* (Garden City, New York: Doubleday & Co., 1974), 54.

9. Gregory Michael Smith, *The Fire in Their Eyes: Spiritual Mentors for the Christian Life* (New York: Paulist Press, 1984), back cover.

10. Ibid., 39.

11. See Sandra De Gidio, O.S.M. *RCIA: The Rites Revisited* (Minneapolis: Winston Press, 1984), 15-29.

3. The Rite of Entrance

The rite of entrance symbolizes the journey of the converting person from the period of inquiry to the time of instruction.

One of my most vivid childhood memories is of my longing to become a Boy Scout. The local Boy Scout group met next-door in the church my father pastored. Every Friday evening for years I watched the bigger boys come to the Scout meeting decked out in their spiffy Scout uniforms. I hung around the church peeking in the windows at the games, the serious discussion, and the fun this society of fortunate people enjoyed. When they left on their scouting trips, I was there to help them pack and to wave goodbye. And when they returned, I was there to welcome them, help them unpack, and listen to their camping stories with wonderment and jealousy. I kept track of the months, the weeks, and even the days as I approached the magic age of twelve.

Finally, the day came when I could join the Scouts. The meeting for the induction of the new Boy Scouts was held in the woods behind the church, in an open patch of grass by a small stream. It was a warm summer evening, a gentle breeze was blowing, and the sky was filled with numerous stars. We sat around a sparkling fire, singing songs and listening to stories about selfless Boy Scouts becoming men of honor and influence. Then, in a solemn ceremony of induction, our names were called out and we stepped forward to hear the words of welcome and admonition, to receive the Boy Scout handshake and then to join the other scouts in the Scout's oath. My dream had come true. I could now begin a new journey, a journey within, a journey of learning and fun, a journey of challenges and accomplishments in the Boy Scout community.

The rite of entrance into the Boy Scout troop is similar in form and meaning to the rite of welcome into the church. As passage rites, both symbolize a movement from one period of development to another. Every journey is characterized by turning points. Acknowledging the significance of these turning points, we have created rites to symbolize and commemorate them, and rightly so. Consider the rites that have developed around birthdays, graduations, engagements, weddings, and anniversaries. These rites shape and enhance our personal histories. Without them life would be less exciting and less secure. Similarly, our development in faith is characterized by rites of religious passage that embody and communicate the event they symbolize.

THE BIBLICAL BACKGROUND

The formal rite of welcome was created in the second and third centuries. Because this ritual signifies entrance into the church, its biblical background lies in the use of ritual in the Scripture. Consequently, to understand the significance of the rite of entrance, we must study Scripture and grapple with the meaning of ritual in worship.[1]

First, a distinction must be made between ritual and ritualism. According to Amos ritualism is abhorrent to God. "I hate, I despise your feasts, and I take no delight in your solemn assemblies. Even though you offer me burnt offerings and cereal offerings, I will not accept them, and the peace offerings of your fatted calf I will not look upon. Take away from me the noise of your songs; to the melody of your harps I will not listen. But let justice roll down like waters, and righteousness like an everflowing stream" (Amos 5:21-24). Jesus was equally severe toward the ritualism of the Pharisees: " 'I desire mercy, and not sacrifice' " (Matt. 9:13).

Ritualism, whether in the Old Testament, New Testament, or the present is the performance of a rite without meaning and intention. Amos and Jesus condemned those who performed the motions of the rite without a corresponding internal experience, without allowing the meaning of those rites to shape their belief or life. In ritualism the meaning of the rite has no effect on the person either during the performance of the rite or afterwards. The Scriptures condemn ritualism but not ritual as such. Ritual is an external action united with an internal intention, giving expression to an internal experience. It orders and organizes internal feelings and provides a structure through which faith and commitment are expressed.

Liturgical writers recognize that worship is a ritual context in which an encounter between God and his people takes place.[2] Biblically, the concept of God encountering his people through a visible and tangible form is rooted in the incarnation. God did not become present in a bodyless, spiritual form. Rather, God became present in human flesh and blood, in the person of Jesus Christ. In this encounter God incarnate lived among us, died on the wood of the cross, was placed in a tomb, and rose from the dead. This literal, historical, and tangible form of communication affirms the use of tangible, visible forms through which God continues to encounter us. The rite of entrance then, assuming it is done in faith and with intention, is a visible, audible, organized expression of the relationship established between God and his people. In worship a relationship is established, maintained, repaired, and transformed. So worship creates spiritual life, brings a spiritual relationship into being, and establishes communication.

Worship encounters that create relationships are representations of Christ expressed through recitation and drama. Representation is the means through which God's historical action of salvation is contemporized. This is true in both Old and New Testament worship. In Old Testament worship, God's deliverance from Egypt is made contemporary through both word and rite (see Exod. 24:1–8). In New Testament worship, following the same pattern, God's saving action is made present through the preaching of the Word and the celebration of the Eucharist (see Acts 2:42). In each case what is made present is the saving event. In the Old Testament, it is the redemption from Egypt; in the New Testament, it is redemption from the powers of evil by the crucifixion. All services of Christian worship are rooted in the Christ event, the one single event that makes a relationship with God possible. In worship the historical Christ event is represented and made contemporaneous.

The rite of entrance needs to be seen as a recitation and drama of the Christ event and the relationship established through that event with the people of God, the church. Recitation and drama reach the whole person through a variety of communication channels. The relationship to God already established in faith is strengthened.

The rite of entrance, then, is an important stage in the journey of faith because of what it says and demands. It says the gospel. It says it in words and in gestures. It orders and organizes a spiritual experience. But it also demands. It demands faith, intention, response. Worship, like a coin, has two sides. In worship, God speaks and acts. But in worship we must respond to God and to each other. This form evokes, elicits, and defines the inner response of the human heart. Without that inner response, the form is ritualism; with the inner response, it is ritual in the biblical and best meaning of the term. Thus, God speaks and acts through the rite of entrance to welcome the converting person into the church.

THE EXPERIENCE OF THE EARLY CHURCH

No detailed description of the rite of entrance has been recorded by church fathers. However, sufficient evidence demonstrates that the rite was in existence in the third century. In *The Apostolic Tradition,* Hippolytus depicts a rite of entrance: "Those who come forward for the first time to hear the Word shall be brought to the teachers [at the house] before all the people come in. And let them be examined as to the reason why they have come forward [to the Faith]. And those who bring them shall bear witness for them whether they are able to hear."[3]

Several decades after Hippolytus wrote, more evidence of the rite of entrance is given by Origen, the head of a Christian school in Alexandria, in his reference to the rite of admission for those who are prepared to move into the period of instruction from the period of inquiry. Writing to Celsus, a pagan philosopher who had attacked Christianity, Origen defended the Christian approach to maturation against that of the philosophers. He claimed that the philosophers talked to anyone who would listen and thus had no organized way of leading their hearers into truth. By comparison the Christians had a series of graduated steps that led a person into the virtuous life. These steps included the inquiry and the period of instruction, connected by a rite of entrance for those who were "receiving admission."[4] Additional proof of the existence of the rite of entrance in the early church is given by Augustine in *On the Catechising of the Uninstructed.* Here he describes the initiate as one who "is to be solemnly signed and dealt with in accordance with the custom of the church."[5]

Unfortunately, the church fathers did not write an exposition on the meaning of the rite of entrance. Nevertheless, they mention certain specific rituals. These rituals, together with an understanding of their meaning, provide significant clues to what the rite of entrance may have meant to the early Christians.

The most important of these rites was the rite of signation. This rite—the sign of the cross made on the forehead of each candidate—signified that the candidate now belonged to Christ, whose sign (the cross) he or she bore. This mark set the new convert apart as Christian even before baptism. A second rite, the imposition of hands, usually accompanied the signation. Since this gesture appears to have been repeated after every meeting of the catechumens, it is not known whether it signified the act of being brought under the care of the church or whether it was a rite of exorcism. In either case it pointed to a relationship of dependence upon the church: the one who comes to Christ must come to Christ through the church.

The custom of giving salt to the new candidate originated in North Africa. While a variety of meanings may have been assigned to this rite, it essentially served as a sign of hospitality, a welcome into the community of faith. It may also have symbolized the calling to be the salt of the earth or reminded the candidate of purification and wisdom. Finally, there is also some evidence of the rite of breathing. Although references to this rite are scarce, the meaning may be related to blowing away evil spirits and receiving the Holy Spirit.[6]

What is of primary importance here is that these rites supported the main emphasis of the rite of entrance, which was to signify renouncing evil, paganism, and the old life and crossing over into a new life in Christ and the church. Consequently, the rite of entrance is seen as a type of the Exodus or even as a conception in the womb of the church.[7] The experience of the early church in the rite of entrance, together with the biblical understanding of ritual, has given shape and meaning to the modern restoration of this rite.

APPLICATION TO CONTEMPORARY EVANGELISM

The text of the RCIA suggests that the essence of the ancient rite of entrance can be captured in the following elements:

—First instruction
—Opening dialogue
—First promise
—Exorcism and renunciation of non-Christian worship (optional)
—The signing of the senses
—Giving the new name (optional)
—Entrance into the church.

The rite begins as the converting people assemble at the back of the sanctuary or in the narthex. After the service of entrance, they will walk into the sanctuary and take a seat among the faithful to symbolize their actual entrance among the people of God. This service begins in the back of the sanctuary with the first instruction, in which the celebrant (minister) welcomes the new converts and their sponsors to the church and the journey into Christ now being taken.

Then, in the opening dialogue, the celebrant asks each candidate to give his or her name and to state why he or she is there and what is desired. This is followed by the first promises. In this part of the service, the celebrant proclaims the gospel and the promise of new life to those who receive Jesus Christ as personal Lord and Savior.

Next, in the exorcism and renunciation of non-Christian worship, the celebrant calls upon the converting persons to renounce all association with pagan rites and habits and to be committed solely to the worship of the triune God. This may or not be accompanied by a symbol such as blowing the breath upon the candidate or some other appropriate gesture that symbolizes evil put to flight. (A particularly useful symbol in primitive cultures, this could be adapted to Western culture as well.)

In the signing of the senses, the candidate steps forward to receive the sign of the cross on the forehead, ears, eyes, lips, breastbone and shoulder. This action symbolizes that the whole person belongs to Christ. After this, in the giving of a new name, the celebrant may ascribe a Christian name to the candidate. This is especially effective in pagan cultures in which an original name may be associated with a pagan deity or power. However, it is also applicable in the West. Finally comes the entry into the church. The candidates are invited to enter into the church and to be seated among the faithful. (In keeping with the ancient tradition the nonbaptized Christian may remain in worship for the liturgy of the Word, but may not receive the bread and wine until after baptism.)[8]

These various steps in the rite of entrance verbalize and dramatize the action of moving from the condition of unbelief to belief. Both the action of God and the human response are central. For example, the action of God is verbally climaxed in the first promise when the leader reviews what

God has done to provide salvation. The exorcism and renunciation of non-Christian worship dramatically proclaims the candidates' allegiance to Jesus Christ.

Liturgical evangelism, unlike other kinds of evangelism, brings the converting person into Christ and the church through periods of increasing intensity and commitment. The growth and development of the converting person from one period to the other is signified by rites of passage. The rite of entrance into the stage of instruction is the first of three passage rites. Consequently, what will be said of passage rites here will be equally applicable to the two other passage rites, the rite of election and the rite of initiation.

Modern Protestants, evangelicals, and even some Catholics of the Western world are hampered in their understanding of ritual by the narrow view of reality inherited from the Enlightenment. The rationalistic view of life tends to disdain prelogical, intuitive, and ceremonial forms of communication. It looks on ritual as primitive, akin to magic, and intellectually inferior. However, this disregard for ritual as a form of communication is changing. First, current sociological studies now recognize the importance rites play in every society. A rite is defined as "any standardized procedure used by groups to enunciate or to strengthen a belief and thereby to produce some desired end."[9] Sociologists rightly point out that the entire structure and functioning of our society is based on rites. The way we welcome the birth of a baby, greet guests, apply for a job, marry off our children, bury the dead, and install public officials are only a few examples of the role rites play in our everyday life.

Second, indications that the importance of ritual is being recovered is found in current psychological studies. They point to the importance ritual plays in the changes that take place in life. A pioneer in the field, Arnold Van Gennep, suggests that rites can be categorized under three headings: the rites of separation, the rites of transition, and the rites of incorporation.[10] In some cases all three of these aspects occur in a single rite, while in other cases one or the other is emphasized more fully. Burial is a rite of separation; marriage is a rite of transition; the rite of entrance is a rite of incorporation. These rites, whether simple and unadorned or elaborate and filled with pomp and ceremony, are increasingly recognized as essential to a healthy people and society.

Now we must ask, what does a rite do? What actually happens as the result of a ritual? A rite is a way of approaching mystery—the mystery of birth, marriage, or death. In the case of worship or of liturgical evangelism in particular, a rite enables us to approach the mystery of God, to establish a relationship with him.

A passage rite must convey what it means. In the case of the rite of entrance, the rite itself means entrance into the body of Christ, welcome into the community of the Savior. In the rite of entrance, the mystery of conversion is acted out. The converting persons stand apart from the body of Christ (separation), renounce Satan (transition), and finally take their place among the faithful (incorporation). This external ordering of the rite of entrance symbolizes and thus realizes the inner resolve of the converting person to forsake the kingdom of evil for the kingdom of God.

A rite may be seen as a communication that takes place on a deeper level than cognitive understanding. It reaches into the heart, into the deepest levels of human personality, where it resonates. For example, in the early seventeenth century, a debate over the importance of this emotional appeal ensued between Johann Sebastian Bach and Johann August Ernesti. Ernesti, who was a pioneer in the critical examination of Scripture, insisted that students should study more and sing less. Bach countered that the biblical text was designed to release within the reader an intense sort of spiritual activity—faith. Ernesti chose religion—a rationalistic, analytical, intellectual perspective. Bach choose faith—an intuitive, experiential perspective.[11]

In the ensuing years, the rational emphasis of Ernesti became dominant and the mystical dimension of faith went into decline. But now, in the context of the communications revolution and the discovery of the function of the right side of the brain as the "poetic" side of human personality,[12] the wisdom of Bach is making a comeback. The rite of entrance is a form of communication in the tradition of Bach—an intuition, a form that evokes an inner experience of faith. For this reason the rite of entrance will draw on the mystical sensibilities not only of the persons involved, but also of the whole congregation.

Regis Duffy, a renowned Catholic teacher and writer, has rightly pointed out that "the church has never simply taught the paschal mystery. Rather she has always invited and enabled Christians to participate in that mystery."[13] The Protestant tradition has reversed the ancient Christian tradition of *lex orandi, lex credendi* (the law of worship is the law of belief) and assumed that belief must precede worship. We have unsuccessfully tried to teach mystery, rather than to let it be intuited through the rites of worship.

The mystery in the rite of entrance touches on the meaning of life from the Christian perspective. It points to the most fundamental issue of evangelism—repenting, turning away from evil, and entering into a new life in Christ and the community of the church. It explains life at its deepest level and brings a person into the experience of community. When the whole congregation participates in the rite of initiation, as it should, the result is an annual ceremony of conversion and nurturing in the Christian faith. This resembles the annual revival meetings held in rural churches. Not only are new converts brought into the church, but established members are also called into a renewed dedication to the faith and to the church.

The rite of entrance had its origin in the early church, in which it was used to bring a person from the period of inquiry to the period of instruction and training in the faith. And we have seen its significance in the broader light of the meaning of ritual.[14] Originally, it was not a mere ritualistic form, nor does it need to be today. It brings a person into the mystery of the faith, confirms the covenant God is making with him or her and elicits a response. It is not a gimmick or a device, but a sacramental embodiment of the relationship being established between God and the people. It presents Christ as victor over sin and death, incorporates a converting person into the worshiping community and the mysteries of salvation and represents a step into a new period of conversion—instruction in the faith.

NOTES

1. See Leonel L. Mitchell, *The Meaning of Ritual* (Harrisburg, PA: Morehouse Publishing, 1987) and James Shaughnessy, ed., *The Roots of Ritual* (Grand Rapids, MI: Eerdmans, 1973).
2. See Shaughnessy, *Roots of Ritual.*
3. *The Treatise on the Apostolic Tradition of St. Hippolytus of Rome,* p. 23.
4. Origen, *Against Celsus,* bk. III, 51, *The Anti-Nicene Fathers,* ed. A. Cleveland Coxe (Grand Rapids, MI: Eerdmans, 1972), vol. IV., 484.
5. Quoted by Michel Dujarier, *The Rites of Christian Imitation* (New York: Sadlier, 1979), 36.
6. Ibid., 33–39.
7. See Dujarier, "History of the Catechumenate," 19–26.
8. The rite of entrance is reconstructed from biblical and early church sources. Since there is no mention of the rite of entrance in the New Testament, we acknowledge it to be a creation of the church. However, it is based on biblical

principles. For the full text of the rite of entrance, see U. S. Catholic Conference, *Rite of Christian Initiation of Adults: Provisional Text* (Washington, D.C., 1974), 17–27 (hereafter cited as *RCIA*).

9. Harry Holbert Turney-High, *Man and System: Foundations for the Study of Human Relations* (New York: Meredith, 1968), 253–254.

10. Arnold Van Gennep, *The Rites of Passage* (Chicago: The University of Chicago Press, 1960), 11ff.

11. See Gwen Kennedy Neville and John H. Westerhoff III, *Learning Through Liturgy* (New York: The Seabury Press, 1978), 122.

12. For a thorough analysis of the functioning of the right and left sides of the brain, see David G. Myers, *The Human Puzzle: Psychological Research and Christian Belief* (New York: Harper & Row, 1978).

13. Regis A Duffy, O.F.M., *On Becoming a Catholic: The Challenge of Christian Initiation* (San Francisco: Harper & Row, 1984), 86.

14. For a classic analysis of ritual, see Victor W. Turner, *The Ritual Process* (Chicago: Aldine Publishing Co., 1969).

4. The Catechumenate

The Catechumenate is a period during which the new convert receives personal instruction and discipleship in the Christian faith.

I first met Steve in the third meeting of my course on Christian thought in 1968, the year I began teaching at Wheaton College. Steve distinguished himself that day in class by publicly announcing that he did not believe in God. "We work on two different presuppositions," he declared. "You believe in God, I do not." Immediately after class I caught his eye and shouted, "Steve, wait for me. I want to talk with you."

I found out that Steve was a Jewish boy who was brought up in the streets of Brooklyn. At an early age, he was streetwise and tough. Like Saul of Tarsus, his life was turned around because someone dared to witness to him. Unlike Saul, he was turned into an instant celebrity. "Look," they said, "at what the gospel can do. Why, it can take a kid right off the streets and instantly transform him." Steve was a trophy, an evangelical success story, a miracle. In no time at all, he was the featured speaker in youth gatherings and in Sunday night services in the New York area. People were so impressed with him that they raised enough money to send him off to a Christian college.

But now, several years later, Steve was not only an unbeliever, but a cynic. What happened to this trophy? Why the change? In one of many intimate conversations, Steve confessed that he had never been baptized. "Why?" I asked.

"The commitment was more than I could handle," he admitted. "Were you ever instructed in the faith?" I asked. "Not really," he answered. I have often wondered whether it was the lack of a catechumenate that caused Steve to lose faith. Was Steve unable to grow in the faith because he had not experienced a period of nurturing, because his was a premature birth?

The catechumenate, a time of formation and instruction, is the womb-like period for the newly conceived Christian. It is a time to be nurtured, cared for, and formed by the Word. For the candidate it is still a time of searching. But unlike the period of inquiry when the search goes on outside the Christian community, this is a time when the search occurs within the Christian community.

BIBLICAL BACKGROUND

I once visited a large Baptist church in the South where baptisms were conducted after every service of worship for the people who responded on that day to the preaching of Christ. The argument for immediate baptism was drawn from Acts, from the accounts in which conversion and baptism apparently occur without any intervening time. However, I believe a closer study of these texts brings instant baptism into question and supports the argument for a time of instruction between conversion and baptism.

First, in Acts, chapter 2, in response to Peter's Pentecost sermon, "those who received his word were baptised, and there were added that day about three thousand souls" (Acts 2:41). Many interpret the baptism following Pentecost as a baptism without preparation, a baptism that occurred on the day of Pentecost. The text, however, may be understood differently. The term "that day" may refer to the eschatalogical day, the day of the new beginning, which was inaugurated by the work of Christ and first experienced on the day of Pentecost.

Furthermore, a discernable journey toward conversion appears to be manifest in various stages. The claim of the text is that Peter "testified with many other words." While these "many other words" could have been stated in a single day, they could just as likely be spread over a longer period time. This interpretation allows for a sequence of time between conversion and baptism.[1]

Something like the period of growth assumed in the catechumenate may be implied by the qualification that those who *received* his word were baptized. These words may suggest that after repentance and turning away from one's former life, one entered into a period of training, a period of living the Christian life and learning the faith before baptism.

The same possible sequence is found in a second highly visible example, namely that of the conversion of the Ethiopian Eunuch recorded in Acts, chapter 8, verses 26–40. Again, on the surface the conversion of the Eunuch appears to have been instantaneous, without any preliminary preparation. However, a closer reading of the text suggests that while the baptism did take place immediately after conversion, a longer period of preparation preceded the conversion. The Eunuch was already deeply rooted in the religion of Israel; he was reading the book of Isaiah; and he sensed that he did not yet understand what his heart grasped. Consequently, God directed Philip to go to him and to witness in such a way that the journey into faith that he had been making for some time would take a dramatic turn. Thus, even the Ethiopian's account presupposes a journey toward baptism rather than an abrupt and instant baptism.

Augustine comments on this text, defending the notion

of a journey toward baptism and rejecting the possibility of a baptism occurring without regard to the basic teachings of the gospel. He suggests that Philip did in fact present the Eunuch with the basic teachings of the Christian faith.

Indeed, to preach Christ is to state everything that must be believed about Christ, not only whose Son He is, whence begotten according to His divinity, whence according to His flesh, what He suffered and why He suffered, what is the virtue of His resurrection, what gift of the Spirit He promised and gave to the faithful; but also what kind of members He, the Head, seeks, ordains, loves, frees from bonds of sin, and leads to eternal life and glory. When these facts are related, sometimes more briefly and with restriction, other times more comprehensively and in greater detail, Christ is being preached. At the same time, what pertains to faith is not left unsaid.[2]

Further support for an evangelism that consists of various stages of commitment and knowledge can be argued from the text of Hebrews. A journey that goes beyond the preliminary hearing of the gospel is implied in the distinction made between milk and solid food in Hebrews, chapter 5, verses 12–14. This sense of a journey is buttressed by the admonition to "leave the elementary doctrines of Christ and go on to maturity" (Heb. 6:1). Certainly, this text implies stages, steps, growth, process, development. Christians, like the newborn babes, are not to remain in arrested development. No, like a parent, the writer of Hebrews was calling newborn babes into a journey toward maturity, into a dissatisfaction with a Christian faith that remains arrested.

These illustrations suggesting that newly born Christians were put through a period of training before baptism are reinforced by the catechetical materials of the New Testament. They imply a period of time for learning and adapting to the new way of life that baptism demands (see Col. 3: 8–4:12; Eph. 4:22–6:19; 1 Pet. 1:1–4:11; 1 Pet. 4:12–5:14; James 1:1–4:10).[3] Philip Carrington, in *The Primitive Christian Catechesis,* points to four emphases in the New Testament catechetical material: (1) *deponenter* (putting off evil), (2) *subjecti* (submission to God and each other), (3) *vigilate* (watching and praying), and (4) *resistite* (resisting the devil). For example, this pattern of teaching is readily seen in Ephesians: (1) "Put on the new nature, created after the likeness of God in true righteousness and holiness. . . . Therefore, putting away falsehood" (Eph:4:24–25), (2) "Be subject to one another" (Eph 5:21), (3) "Put on the whole armor of God" (Eph 6:11) (4) "That you may be able to stand against the wiles of the devil" (Eph. 6:11).[4]

The New Testament catechesis touches on attitudes and values that go to the very heart of Christian development. They describe the journey from paganism to Christian faith. Conversion is a movement away from a former way of life, from former commitments and values, to a new life and new values. The convert journeys into a new community of people, a people who live in submission to God and each other, battle the forces of evil, and stand against the devil in the name of Jesus, the victor over the devil's domain and power.

Instant conversion accompanied by an immediate ability to do the will of God is not the norm. Being born into this community takes time, time for formation, time for the acquisition of new values, time for the transfer of allegiance from worldly powers to the power of Christ working in and through his body, the church. However, while the New Testament texts cited previously suggest the existence of some kind of period of formation between conversion and baptism, no evidence documents the formal development of the catechumenate until the third century.

THE EXPERIENCE OF THE EARLY CHURCH

Unfortunately, none of the third-century writers provides us with a detailed explanation of the catechumenate stage. However, beginning with Hippolytus in Rome around 220 A.D., we can gain specific but undeveloped insights into the content of the catechumenate.

Let a catechumen be instructed for three years. But if a man be earnest and persevere well in the matter, [let him be received], because it is not the time that is judged, but the conduct.

Each time the teacher finishes his instruction let the catechumens pray by themselves apart from the faithful. And let the women stand in the assembly by themselves [apart from the men], both the baptised women and the women catechumens.

But after the prayer is finished the catechumens shall not give the kiss of peace, for their kiss is not yet pure. But the baptised shall embrace one another, men with men and women with women. But let not men embrace women.

Moreover let all the women have their heads veiled with a scarf but not with a veil of linen only, for that is not a covering.

After the prayer [of the catechumens] let the teacher lay hands upon them and pray and dismiss them. Whether the teacher be an ecclesiastic or a layman let him do the same.

If any [one being a] catechumen should be apprehended for the Name, let him not be anxious about martyrdom. For if he suffer violence and be put to death before baptism, he shall be justified having been baptised in his own blood.[5]

The setting described by Hippolytus is that of a Christian community at worship. While this is more than likely a Sunday setting, the community frequently gathered for worship during the week, so it may describe what would happen on days other than Sunday as well. In the third century, worship consisted of two major parts, the liturgy of the Word and the liturgy of the Eucharist. Catechumens were admitted to the liturgy of the Word but dismissed before that of the Eucharist, which only those who had been baptized could attend. Hippolytus describes the place of the catechumen in the liturgy of the Word.

Hippolytus reveals much about the nature of the catechumenate. The period of instruction could extend as long as three years. If, as Hippolytus suggests, a person's faith and conduct showed more rapid formation, he or she proceeded more quickly to entrance into the full life of the church.

The instruction referred to by Hippolytus is the sermon that was intended for the baptized as well as the unbaptized. While we do not know the specific content of these sermons, we do know that they were drawn from the Scripture. For example, the description given by Justin Martyr in 150 A.D. provides insight into early third-century preaching. "The memoirs of the apostles or the writings of the prophets are read, as long as time permits . . . , when the reader has finished, the president in a discourse urges and invites us to the imitation of these noble things."[6] The emphasis appears to fall not only on knowledge of truth, but also on the way of life that the faith demands. Preaching in worship is much more than information; it has to do with the formation of values and way of life.

After the instruction the catechumens were separated from the baptized for a prayer time. The separation probably related to the different experiential stages of the baptized and unbaptized. The catechumens were in the process of learning how to pray. Having been separated from those who already knew how to pray, they received a greater freedom to be instructed in prayer and to pray aloud without feeling self-conscious.

Further distinction was made between the baptized and the unbaptized by withholding the kiss of peace from the catechumen. The kiss of peace was a sign indicating that since peace with God was made through Jesus Christ, peace also existed between God's people. It was signified by a handshake or embrace with the accompanying words "The peace of the Lord be with you." While today the withholding of the kiss of peace from the catechumen seems odd, it must be remembered that the catechumen is on a journey and not everything in the Christian church was instantly available.

However, at the conclusion of the catechumen's prayer, the catechumens did receive the counterpart to the kiss of peace—a special prayer from their instructor and the imposition of hands. While we have no record of this prayer, which was extemporaneous, we can assume it was a prayer for the catechumens, for their growth in Christ, for courage and strength to live the Christian life in the context of a pagan world. This laying on of hands was partly an exorcism and partly a blessing.

The practice of exorcism ought not to be seen as unusual, since the early church was characterized by an appropriate charismatic sense. It was quite common to anoint with oil and pray for the power of the Spirit to drive away evil influences. The imposition of hands was, as we will see, a vital part of Christian formation in the third century. It proclaimed the power of the Holy Spirit in the community of the church to support the new believer's pilgrimage to a life characterized by Christian conduct.

Further information about the content of instruction for the catechumen may be garnered from the images used by the church fathers to describe the catechumen's journey. Third-century fathers such as Tertullian, Cyprian, and Commodian frequently described the catechumenate as analo-

gous to the training soldiers had to undergo. First, a person
had to go through stages of development to become a soldier. The would-be soldier began as a *tiro,* a novice who had
to spend time in an apprenticeship learning how to use his
weapons and equipment before becoming a soldier. Once his
proficiency had been proven, an oath to serve, even at the
cost of his life, was taken. This oath was sealed by the tattoo
of his superior.

In similar fashion the Christian convert had to renounce
his or her pagan background and enter an apprenticeship in
which training in the weapons of God against Satan was
given. Once the recruit passed the test, admittance to the
church through initiation was accompanied by the seal of the
Holy Spirit. From that time on, the convert was to do battle
with Satan and the forces of evil. This image of military
training points to the *Christus victor* theme that dominates the
worldview of the third century. Christ the victor over sin,
death, and the dominion of Satan was calling recruits into his
community, the church, the sign of his victory in the world.
Their calling was to live the life of victory over sin in the
context of a pagan world. And through this new life, witness
was made to the powers of evil that their defeat had already
been made certain.

A second highly popular analogy for the catechumenate
is the Exodus of the Old Testament. This is a favorite theme,
particularly for Origen of Alexandria. He compared the
effort to abandon paganism and accept Christ to Israel's de-
parture from Egypt for the promised land. The crossing of
the Red Sea was analogous to their rite of welcome into the
church. Next, the catechumenate was likened to the sojourn
of Israel in the wilderness. Here the catechumens heard the
law of God, and as with Moses, the glory of God was revealed
to them. When the catechumens passed through this time of

testing and growth, their rite of initiation would be like passing through Jordan River to the promised land.[7] In this image the journey, periods of development, and passage rites are emphasized. And surely the image of the Exodus was meant to encourage the pilgrim by the example to endure to the end. It is not merely incidental that the journey of Israel was a journey of people together. For the journey into Christ, like Israel, is the journey of a people who support, assist, and encourage each other on the way.

The third and the most popular image of the catechumenate is that of gestation and birth. The analogy here is obvious. The candidate is conceived in the womb of the church by the word of God. And the catechumenate is the period of gestation, the time of formation and development in the womb. This time is concluded by the rite of baptism, which is a birth into the family of God. Born into this new environment, the infant is given tender, loving care, nursed, coddled, and nourished into maturity. This image, like the others, emphasizes formation, development, process, and growth. Furthermore, it stresses new life in the context of family and community. The early church knew no such thing as an individualistic Christianity—it practiced evangelism by, in, and through the community of God's people.

APPLICATION TO CONTEMPORARY EVANGELISM

We turn now from the world of the early church to ask how the ancient catechumenate may be adopted and put to use in liturgical evangelism today. It is, of course, of utmost importance to retain the catechumenate. The formation that goes on during the catechumenate is an integral part of the conversion process because it solidifies what began in the inquiry stage. Like the child being formed in the womb, the new convert experiences a period of gestation and prenatal development, a necessary stage of birth.

A unique feature of the catechumenate then and now is that it is a formation that occurs within the church. This is evangelism within community, not beyond the borders of the church. The instructor is not an individual, but the whole community. In this way the local church brings the new convert into its communal experience of the living presence and power of the risen Christ.

Modern discussions about the role of the catechumenate in evangelism revolve around three issues in particular: the content communicated to the catechumen, the setting in which this content is expressed, and the rituals that embody and aid the process of Christian formation. First, the content of the catechumenate stresses growth in Christ through worship, study of the word, and social action. This structure appeals to the convert emotionally and intellectually and conveys values that shape action in the world. *Formation,* not information, is the key concern. This does not mean that content and knowledge are unimportant. Rather, the emphasis is on information that gives birth to Christian experience, to a Christian perspective, and to a Christian way of life. For during the catechumenate, the new convert is formed into a new person in relationship to Christ, to the church as a community of people, and to the world.

It is generally recognized that the experience of worship is fundamental to understanding and to action. In the early church, it was always argued that *lex orandi* (the rule of worship), preceded *lex credendi* (the rule of faith or knowledge). Both our reflection on the faith and our action because of the faith grow out of our worship.

I always remind my students in theology classes that the

primitive Christian community first experienced the reality of God and salvation, then later, through reflection on that experience, developed their theology. In the modern world, we frequently reverse that order by teaching theology first and expecting experience and action to flow from this intellectual understanding. However, educators are now calling us back to the wisdom of the early church fathers. Their argument that you cannot know what you have not experienced is now more widely received than at any other time during this century.

Worship maintains and deepens the relationship that has been established with God. The new convert develops a relationship to transcendence, to the spiritual side of reality, to the mystery that is fundamental to the universe. This cannot be taught in an intellectual way. Relationship with God through prayer, through the spiritual hearing of his word, and through interaction with community cannot be learned in a classroom lecture or put on a blackboard diagram. It has to happen. It has to be experienced.

After the experience of worship, reflection and cognitive development can begin. For example, to discuss the transcendence of God the Father, the incarnation of God the Son, or the power of the Holy Spirit in the context of the action of Father, Son, and Holy Spirit in worship keeps doctrinal convictions from being mere intellectual propositions. The same can be said for the new convert's relationship to the world. The study of the social dimension of prayer or scripture, such as the writings of the prophets or Jesus' Sermon on the Mount, has greatest impact when related to worship. Active response to God's call to Christian responsibility in the world inevitably arises out of true worship.

The second issue for modern Christians is the setting of the catechumenate: both the Sunday morning experience of worship and an additional meeting during the week devoted to the formation of the baptismal candidate. In the Sunday morning service of worship, the new convert learns how to participate in the central experience of the Christian community, corporate worship. As in the ancient church, new converts are not admitted to the table of the Lord. Consequently, formation in worship takes place for them in preaching of the word and in the prayer life of the community.

For example, assume that the people of a particular church, or at least a dedicated core of people, are committed to an evangelism through community in the catechumenate. What then is their course of action? What do they do for the new convert? First, formation within the Sunday morning setting of word and prayer will best occur in the larger context of the church year. In the church year, the life of Christ is celebrated through a series of liturgical events that have the power to shape Christian experience and form the new convert's understanding of Christian faith, spirituality, and way of life.

Imagine for a moment that you are a new convert to the faith. You were converted during the summer or fall, the rite of welcome celebrated your entrance into the church sometime before Advent, and now at Advent your formation within the catechumenate begins. What you will experience in the worship life of the church between Advent and Easter is an introduction to the core of Christian faith. In Advent you will experience the hope and longing of Israel and the world for the coming of the Messiah. At Christmas you will be taken into the mystery of the incarnation. You will experience the birth of our Lord, "God with us" (Matt. 1:23), you will sing with Mary, "My soul magnifies the Lord" (Luke 1:46), and you will enter the praise of Simeon, "Mine eyes have seen my salvation" (Luke 2:30). And then, with the wise men on Epiphany you will fall down and worship Jesus. During Lent you will enter into the experience of Christ's death; with the community you gather on Ash Wednesday and hear the words, "Remember that you are dust and to dust you shall return." With the community of God's people, you enter into the spirituality of suffering. By participating in fasting, prayer, and almsgiving, you spiritually enter Jesus' journey toward Jerusalem and his death. During Holy Week you enter the experience of the community of Jesus' followers as they move from the glorious entrance into Jerusalem on Palm Sunday to the Last Supper on Maundy Thursday and the trial, crucifixion, and burial on Good Friday. And with the Christians around the world, you wait for the celebration of the glorious resurrection of our Lord, the victor over sin and death, which you celebrate during the Easter season.

What is the value of experiencing the life of Christ through the church year? Gwen Neville and John Westerhoff III in *Learning Through the Liturgy* emphasize the power of experience to shape perspective. "Through the power of symbolic actions we order our experience; through the use of symbolic narrative we explain our lives. Ritual operates on those levels of existential reality that undergird the conceptual."[8] This ritual of the church year, in the drama of telling and acting out the life of Christ, powerfully shapes the life of the new convert and of the community of faith in terms of the pattern of Christ's birth, death, and resurrection. In this way the week-to-week worship life of the church draws the new convert into the life of Christ, which the church continues to live out as the sign of redemption in a secular world.

In addition to the liturgical life of the church, new converts may be set apart in specific groups in which special attention is given to their formation in knowledge, spirituality, and responsibility for the world. Here, in this more informal setting, any number of subjects may be studied. Some churches offer actual courses of study on the Bible, Christian doctrine, and Christian social responsibility. At the heart of this study, however, lie the Apostles' Creed and its teaching on Christian thought, the Lord's Prayer and its teaching on prayer, and the Sermon on the Mount and its teaching on Christian social responsibility. All three of these areas emphasize not only information, but formation. The catechumen forms a Christian mind, a Christian heart, and a Christian character. The setting of study, discussion, and application in a small group experience complements the experience of worship.

A third current issue is the rituals and rites that express in action what is being learned in the catechumenate. Ritualizing a truth causes that truth to be experienced in a way that mere discussion cannot. For example, in the area of doctrine, Sandra De Gidio writes about her struggle to find a way to ritualize a lesson on the Trinity. She decided to relate it to the sign of the cross, a ritual performed regularly in liturgical churches. One of her students wrote the following response to that experience in a journal.

Two events stand out as significant, and one was far more meaningful than the other. The more meaningful one, which was a deeply moving experience, was learning and doing for the first time the sign of the cross. I was especially touched to have it described as a prayer. The feelings I felt were so powerful that I have only done the sign of the cross twice, once at our meeting and once again that night as a final prayer before going to sleep. As I have thought about my feelings, I think they relate to three things. First, I find the simplicity of the prayer makes it very powerful. Its message is not confused in a lot of words. Second, the prayer involves physical action. It makes me feel more involved, more committed. Finally, because of this action I feel I am making a visible sign that I believe in God and that I am Catholic. The sign of the cross is a uniquely Catholic act and I find this visible declaration of the church to be particularly significant. I said I have prayed this prayer only twice. I've done this in part not to diminish the feelings I felt during those first two times, but to save another symbol of my initiation until Easter.[9]

While this illustration may not be applicable to Protestant churches that do not use the sign of the cross, it shows the powerful effect of asking the catechumen to find a nonverbal way to express truth—drawing a symbol of the trinity or other doctrines of the faith may have a similar effect. In some situations the verbal ritual may be quite effective. It consists of asking for testimony of the effect a truth may have had on one's life.

This principle of doing what has been taught also applies to prayer and social action. It is one thing to study the Lord's Prayer or the Sermon on the Mount. It is another thing actually to pray together and publicly to commit oneself to doing a work of mercy or charity. Teachers of the catechumenate have found that the actual experience shared by the catechumens during their spiritual pilgrimage plays a significant part in their development.

In contrast to my opening example of Steve, who was left on his own after conversion, the catechumenate places the new convert in the womb of the church where the formation of the Christian convert takes place. During this time the assistance of the entire Christian community is marshalled for the formation of the Christian person. The womb of the church forms a person with a new set of relationships—a new relationship with Christ and the church and a new relationship to the world.

NOTES

1. See Michel Dujarier, *A History of the Catechumenate* (New York: Sadlier, 1979), 16-17.
2. Quoted by Michel Dujarier, *A History of the Catechumenate*, 15.
3. See the detailed treatment of these passages in Philip Carrington, *The Primitive Christian Catechesis* (Cambridge: Cambridge University Press, 1940), chap. 4.
4. For this analysis as well as others, see Carrington, *Primitive Christian Catechesis,* especially 42–43.
5. *The Treatise on the Apostolic Tradition of St. Hippolytus of Rome,* 28-30.
6. Justin Martyr, *The First Apology,* 67, in *The Early Christian Fathers* trans. Cyril Richardson (Philadelphia: The Westminster Press, 1956), 287.
7. See Dujarier, *A History,* 66–67.
8. Neville and Westerhoff III, *Learning Through Liturgy,* 132.
9. De Gidio, *RCIA: The Rites Revised,* 47-48.

5. The Rite of Election

The rite of election celebrates the converting person's passage from the catechumenate to the period of intense spiritual preparation before baptism.

Like many other young persons who embark on a seminary education, I was theologically naive. What had meant most to me in my Christian experience was my personal choice to follow after Jesus. But the priority of my personal choice in faith was soon to be challenged. Sitting in a large classroom of students during my first week of seminary, I listened to the theology professor introduce his subject. In his initial lecture, the professor began emphasizing an aspect of Christian theology that was foreign to my background. "You may think," he said, "that you choose God. Despite what you think, I want to argue that one of the most fundamental teachings of scripture is that God always initiates a relationship."

For the next three years, I heard this professor hammer home again and again this theme. "It is God who saves us. In Christ God has done everything that ever needed to be done to save us and bring us to himself. Now, like the hound of heaven, he continues to pursue us to enter into relationship with us and to sustain that relationship." Of course, my professor was not denying the human element of choice. But he insisted, as the rite of election illustrates, that God initially chooses us and calls us to himself. The rite of election is a rite of passage that stresses the choosing role of God in conversion.

THE BIBLICAL BACKGROUND

My seminary professor was right. Scripture does emphasize how God initiates a relationship with his creatures. Consider, for example, how God continued to pursue Adam and Eve after the Fall by making them garments of skin and clothing them as an expression of his love (Gen. 3:21). Then, when the whole human race turned against God, God chose Noah and his family to survive the flood and to populate the earth again (Gen. 6–9). Next, out of this new race of human beings, God chose Abraham and promised to bring forth a nation from his seed, to give this nation a land, and through them to bless the whole world (Gen. 12:13).

In a remarkable passage in Deuteronomy, the book that recites the history of Israel, the Israelites are reminded that they did not choose God, but that God chose them. "The Lord your God has chosen you to be a people for his own possession, out of all the peoples that are on the face of the earth. It was not because you were more in number than any other people that the Lord set his love upon you and chose you, for you were the fewest of all peoples; but it is because the Lord loves you" (Deut. 7:6–8).

God's choice of Israel to be his people is symbolized in a covenantal ritual described in Exodus. The celebration of this ritual must have been an awesome moment for all of Israel. Imagine all the people gathered around the mountain in quiet expectancy. Then Moses stepped forth to act as mediator between them and God. Reading the words of agreement between God and Israel, the people then responded, "all the words which the Lord has spoken we will do." Then Moses, taking the blood of various sacrifices, threw half of the blood over the altar and half over the people in an act of ratification, saying, " 'Behold the blood of the covenant which the Lord has made with you in accordance with all these words' " (Exod. 24:1–8). In this ceremony, which must have trembled with an inexpressible mystery, a kind of rite of election was taking place. For here, at the foot of the mountain, Israel became the people of Yahweh and Yahweh became their God.

But this choosing by God, which is essential to a relationship between God and his creatures in the Old Testament, is a theme that permeates the New Testament as well. Paul reminded his readers at Ephesus that "he chose us in him before the foundation of the world . . . he destined us in love to be his sons through Jesus Christ" (Eph. 1:4–5). And Peter, writing to the Christians dispersed throughout the Roman Empire, referred to them as "chosen and destined by God the Father" (1 Peter 1:2). In another passage Peter makes an obvious comparison of the people of the church to the people of Israel by describing the church as "a chosen race, a royal priesthood, a holy nation, God's own people" (1 Peter 1: 19). As though to reinforce God's choice, Peter reminds these new Christians that "once you were no people but now you are God's people; once you had not received mercy but now you have received mercy" (1 Peter 2:9–10).

While we have no direct ritual in the New Testament that emphasizes God's choosing, God's choosing power is implied in baptism. For example, when Peter wrote to the first-century Christians, he reminded them that Christ died "that he might bring us to God" (1 Peter 1:18). Peter also associated baptism with Christ's death. "Baptism, which corresponds to this, now saves you, not as a removal of dirt from the body but as an appeal to God for a clear conscience, through the resurrection of Jesus Christ" (1 Peter 3:21).

Since no evidence documents a rite of election in the

New Testament, we must assume that this rite, which was developed later, reflected the theme of God's choice implied in baptism. For the theme of baptism is not that I have chosen God. Rather, the essential meaning of baptism is that God has chosen me, because he loves me and wants me to experience the benefit of belonging to his community, the church. Consequently, the rite of election that was developed in the third century emphasizes that those who came to the waters of baptism came because God had chosen them.

THE EXPERIENCE OF THE EARLY CHURCH

The rite of election places those people who have passed through the catechumenate and will now prepare for baptism into a special category. Evidence that such a time was set aside for spiritual preparation before baptism goes all the way back to the first century. In the *Didache* a special fast of one or two days is recommended. Later, in the mid-second century, Justin Martyr reports that both the faith and the behavior of the candidate were scrutinized. And finally, Tertullian, writing at the end of the second century, clearly states that the conversion must be verified before the candidate is baptized. In the early third century, Hippolytus provides us with the first actual reference to this rite of election.[1] "And when they are chosen who are set apart to receive baptism let their life be examined, whether they lived piously while catechumens, whether 'they honoured the widows,' whether they visited the sick, whether they have fulfilled every good work. If those who bring them bear witness to them that they have done thus, [then] let them hear the gospel."[2]

The rite of election is also known as the enrollment of names. In the ancient church, those who had completed the catechumenate and now desired to be approved for baptism were urged to present their names for approval by the church. The seriousness with which this rite was taken may be seen in the following excerpt of a sermon by Ambrose, a bishop in the church during the fourth century:

> Can an athlete enjoy leisure once he has given his name for an event? No, he trains and is anointed every day. He is given a special body; discipline is imposed on him; he has to keep himself chaste. You too have *given in your name* for Christ's interest; you have entered for an event, and its prize is a crown. Practice, train, anoint yourself with the oil of gladness, an ointment that is never used up. Your food should be frugal, without intemperance or self-indulgence. Your drink should be more sparing for fear drunkenness should catch you unawares. Keep your body chaste so as to be fit to wear the crown . . .[3]

Hippolytus indicates two essential parts to the rite of election: the examination and the setting apart. The examination emphasized the style of life. The description of the examination that stresses a sober life, caring for widows and sick, and generally doing good to others sounds very similar to the summary of true religion given by James. "Religion that is pure and undefiled before God and the Father is this: to visit orphans and widows in their affliction, and to keep oneself unstained from the world" (James 1:27). The examination provided an opportunity for the church to discern whether or not the conversion was authentic. To be authentic, the professed conversion had to result in a change of life. It was simply not enough to have a mere intellectual faith. Belief had to be accompanied by a change of life, a change of habits, a change of orientation.

An interesting insight into the change of life expected by the church before baptism is provided by Egira, a Spanish woman who recorded her impressions of the rite of election held in Jerusalem in the fourth century.

> Then the Bishop questions the neighbors of each of the candidates saying, "Does he lead an honest life?" "Does he respect his parents?" "Does he refrain from drunkenness and lying?," covering all the more serious human feelings. If the candidate is recognized in the presence of witnesses, the Bishop writes his name in his own hand. But, if he is accused on some point, the Bishop has him leave, saying, "May he reform, and when he has reformed, he will proceed toward baptism."[4]

A matter of special interest in the examination is the role of the sponsor, who must testify to this change of life. The sponsor, who brought the candidate to the inquiry, stood with the candidate at the rite of welcome, and nurtured the candidate through the catechumenate, must now testify on the candidate's behalf in the rite of election. In the ancient church, the sponsor was usually a friend, a relative, or a neighbor. In the third century, sponsorship did not result from an institutional assignment but grew up out of one-on-one evangelism. Neither was sponsorship a matter of occasional or incidental interest. Rather, the sponsor accompanied the converting person through the whole process of conversion. The sponsor acted as a spiritual director, a personal guide through the conversion journey. Consequently, when the candidate was ready to take the final step toward baptism, the sponsor testified to the seriousness of his or her commitment, Christian faith, and way of life.

The second essential part of the rite of election described by Hippolytus is placing the candidates for baptism into a special group. These candidates now underwent a period of intense spiritual preparation before baptism. The time of this period of preparation corresponded to Lent and culminated in baptism at the great Saturday night vigil that preceded the glorious service of the resurrection on Easter morning.

APPLICATION TO CONTEMPORARY EVANGELISM

As in the ancient church, the rite of election today is considered a turning point in the conversion process. The candidate up to this time has been in a period of testing and training. Now the church, on the testimony of the sponsors, receives the candidate into the final stage of spiritual preparation before baptism. Before the actual celebration of the rite of election, the candidates are examined in the three areas of spiritual growth stressed during the catechumenate—growth in worship, knowledge of the faith, and conduct.

The rite of election, which takes place on the first Sunday of Lent, reflects all the ancient customs. It consists of four parts: (1) the presentation of the candidates, (2) the examination of the candidates, (3) their admission of election, and (4) the prayer for the elect.[5] The rite is a fairly brief ceremony usually conducted after the sermon and before the eucharistic portion of the service.

The rite of election is of course a moment of intense feeling not only for the candidate, but also for the sponsors, relatives, and the whole Christian community. As in the ancient church, the rite of election has been designed to impress upon the candidates that they are here because of God's choosing. As God chose Abraham, Moses, David, Peter, Paul, and John, so God chooses men and women to be members of his church, members of his body on earth.

Imagine, for a moment, that you were converted a year and a half ago, and you have spent a whole year in the catechumenate learning to worship, studying the faith, and having your character formed after Christ. Now, finally, here you are at this crucial turning point in your spiritual journey. The service has begun; the scripture readings emphasizing God's choosing grace have been read; the homily concentrating on the significance of the moment has been preached; and the time has arrived for you to celebrate your election. You wait anxiously as you sit with your sponsor.

The rite of election now begins with the presentation of the candidates to the celebrant. The presenter, a special person who has been in charge of the catechumenate, stands before the celebrant. He says, "I present to you the people who have received Jesus Christ as their personal Savior. These people for more than a year now have been faithful in attendance at the word. They have completed their journey in the catechumenate, they have proven themselves in the faith, in prayer, and in conduct. Now they wish to be admitted to the full life of the church."

As you fight to hold back your feelings, the celebrant says, "Those who are to be chosen by God to become members of his church, please stand." As you are standing together in a special place reserved for the catechumens, the celebrant calls the names of each candidate one by one. As your name is called out, you step forward with your sponsor and join the group you have come to know so well. The celebrant then turns to the sponsors, who one by one give testimony to the new life in Christ. As your sponsor speaks for you, you recall with a sense of satisfaction the journey that brought you to this point in your spiritual pilgrimage.

Next comes the examination. You have already been privately examined and approved by the church. This is a brief and public examination and you are ready for it. Essentially, the celebrant now asks whether you really do wish to become a full member of God's church. "Is this your choice?" You answer that it is. You are then asked, as in the ancient church, to write your name in the book, to enroll yourself among the elect. You step forward, take the pen in your hand, and write your name.

The third part of the rite is the election itself. The celebrant explains that your signature in the book symbolizes that God knows you, that he has chosen you, and that you have responded with a yes. The celebrant now turns toward you and reminds you that you are chosen of God. He then turns to your sponsor and reminds him or her that the responsibility toward you is not over yet. You are again entrusted to the sponsor's care. And the sponsor is admonished to walk close to you through the next several weeks as you prepare for baptism. Then, asking the sponsor to place a hand on your shoulder in the gesture of a caring relationship, the celebrant begins to pray.

The first of the three passage rites, the rite of entrance, carried the new convert from the period of inquiry into the period of the catechumenate. Then, in the womb of the church, the new convert was nourished in faith, in prayer, and in conduct. Next, the rite of election celebrated the conclusion of the catechumenate, confirmed that God had chosen the candidate to be part of his church, and sent the convert into a period of intense spiritual preparation for baptism.

The rite of election, like other rites, is not to be looked upon lightly. Because of its emphasis—God has chosen you —it is an instrument of the Holy Spirit that shapes the experience of the convert. Consequently, it has the effect of drawing the convert up into the message it proclaims, causing the convert to participate in God's choosing not as a reluctant observer, but as an active participant.

NOTES

1. See Michel Dujarier, *The Rites of Christian Initiation,* 93-95.
2. *The Treatise on the Apostolic Tradition of St. Hippolytus of Rome,* 29-30.
3. Quoted from Edward Yarnold, S.J., ed., *The Awe-Inspiring Rites of Initiation: Baptismal Homilies of the Fourth Century* (London: St. Paul Publications, 1972), 14.
4. Quoted from Dujarier, *Rites,* 97.
5. See full text of the rite of election in U.S. Catholic Conference, *RCIA,* 36-43.

6. Purification and Enlightenment

The period of purification and enlightenment, which corresponds to Lent, is a time for spiritual recollection and readiness.

An unusual confrontation with the powers of evil happened to me on a cold January night. I was already tucked away in bed in a deep sleep. The sound of the telephone ringing awakened me. Dragging myself out of bed, I managed a civil hello. "Can you come to my home immediately?" pleaded a voice on the other end. "My daughter Kathy and her boyfriend are here stoned out of their minds and they want you to come." Kathy was one of my students and this was her mother speaking. "Sure," I said, somewhat apprehensively.

The mother met me at the door and quickly ushered me up to the bedroom where Kathy was sprawled out on the bed. She was awake enough to acknowledge my presence. "Go to Bill," she pleaded. "He's struggling with a demonic power and needs your help more than I do."

I stood over Bill, who was lying motionless on a bed in another bedroom. I looked deep into his still eyes. "Demon power," I thought. "Do I really believe in that?" Because I had to make a quick decision, I simply chose to believe, and addressing the demon, I said, "What is your name?"

To my surprise a voice seemed to lift out of Bill's motionless mouth. "Legion," it said.

"I'm here to send you back to hell," I said.

"But Bill will be lonely," the voice retorted.

"No, Christ died for Bill. He will give him the Holy Spirit."

"Why not for me?" the voice said three times.

Stunned by this statement, I finally answered, "You are trying to get me off the subject; I've come to send you back where you belong."

I then held Bill's head and prayed, "In the name of Jesus Christ come out of him." After a number of such prayers, Bill's body went into a series of convulsions. Then his whole body heaved what seemed to be a giant sigh of relief. I felt something leave his body as Bill fell off the bed in a heap on the floor. This scenario continued all night as I wrestled with a power that was obviously beyond me but not beyond the power of Jesus' name. Today Bill and his wife Kathy are committed Christians, active in the local church.

This story seems unlikely in a book on liturgical evangelism. And it is, but only in the sense of its intensity. For during the period of purification and enlightenment, the candidate must deal with the power of evil present in his or her life. While the candidates for baptism will seldom experience the intensity I have described in the case of Bill and Kathy, the reality of evil and its influence is to be confronted during the period of purification and enlightenment.

THE BIBLICAL BACKGROUND

In what some scholars have identified as prebaptismal catechetical material in the New Testament, Paul reminds the Ephesian Christians that "we are not contending against flesh and blood, but against the principalities, against the powers, against the world rulers of this present darkness, against the spiritual hosts of wickedness in heavenly places" (Eph. 6:12).

Paul's warning touches on a recurring theme in the primitive Christian community: the battle waged between the powers of evil and the powers of good. The history of this battle began in the Garden of Eden and will continue until Armageddon. When Adam and Eve chose evil over good, they initiated the contest between good and evil in human history. The writer of Genesis, capturing this dualism between the powers, predicts "enmity between you [Satan] and the woman, and between your seed and her seed; he shall bruise your head, and you shall bruise his heel" (Gen. 3:15).

This bitter struggle between good and evil is seen in the history of God's people, Israel. Even though they entered into covenant with God to become his people, the powers of evil continually drew them away from this agreement. The wandering of Israel in the wilderness for forty years was a prime example of their unfaithfulness. Forgetting the covenant, they turned to other gods. Even after entering into the promised land, they fell away from God again and again. The prophets momentarily brought them back, only to see Israel break covenant with God again.

But the central conflict of this biblical dualism occurs in the life, death, and resurrection of Jesus Christ. For here is the story of how Satan bruised Christ's heel, and Christ crushed the head of Satan. For example, Jesus acted as an exorcist, demonstrating his powers over the demonic. He frequently cast out demons from people (Mark 5:1–20) and claimed he could do so because he had entered into the domain of the wicked one and bound him (Matt. 12:29). In death Christ "disarmed the principalities and powers and made a public example of them, triumphing over them in him" (Col. 2:15). Christ not only conquered the powers of evil in his death, but disarmed them so that they could no longer exercise ultimate control over his creatures and creation. In the resurrection Jesus demonstrated his victory over the powers of death. "Death is swallowed up in victory" (1 Cor. 15:54), no longer a power to be feared, no longer signifying the annihilation of human existence. Rather, because of Jesus' resurrection, the primitive Christian community was urged to break out into song. "O, Death, where is thy victory? O, Death, where is thy sting?" (1 Cor. 15:55).

Even the ascension of Jesus was understood by the primitive church in terms of the struggle between good and evil. For he ascended into heaven not to be absent from his people, but to sit at the right hand of power until all things have been put "under his feet" (Eph. 1:21–23). Finally, the promise of the future is the final and ultimate destruction of Satan and all the powers of evil. In the end, promises the Apocalypse, all powers of wickedness will be "thrown into the lake of fire and brimstone . . . and they will be tormented day and night forever" (Rev. 20:10).

Christ, then, is the hero in the struggle between good and evil. He is the victor over sin, death, and the dominion of evil. But what about now? What about the time between the ascension and the consummation of history? Doesn't evil still exercise its influence over people, families, and nations? Isn't it still a power to be reckoned with?

The ancient church answered these questions in the affirmative. Nevertheless, the church fathers were convinced that the church had been appointed to witness to Christ's powers, to proclaim "the Universe is his!" and "Christ is victor!" Paul, for example, reminded the Ephesians that the victory of Christ over the powers is extended to the world through the church. "Through the church the manifold wisdom of God might now be made known to the principalities and powers in heavenly places" (Eph. 3:10). The church symbolizes the victory of God's redeeming power in a fallen world.

Furthermore, weapons of warfare have been given to the people of the church. "Put on the whole armor of God, that you may be able to stand against the wiles of the devil" (Eph. 6:11). Enumerating these weapons, Paul admonishes his readers to "stand therefore, having girded your loins with truth, and having put on the breastplate of righteousness, and having shod your feet with the equipment of the gospel of peace, above all taking the shield of faith, with which you can quench all the flaming darts of the evil one. And take the helmet of salvation, and the sword of the Spirit, which is the word of God. Pray at all times in the Spirit, with all prayer and supplication. To that end keep alert with all perseverance, making supplication. For all the saints" (Eph. 6:14–18).

This theme of battle with the powers of evil dominates the period of purification and enlightenment. Consequently, this period checks the weapons and readies the warrior. Baptism into Christ is baptism into battle with the powers of evil. But the battle is waged not alone, but with the company of God's people in the church. Therefore, during Lent the converting candidate learns how to draw on the spiritual resources that have been given to the church.

THE EXPERIENCE OF THE EARLY CHURCH

In the early church, two traditions were developed that expressed the power of the church over the powers of evil —the prayer of exorcism and the presentations in which the creed and the Lord's prayer were handed down. The first of these, the exorcisms, is described by Hippolytus.

Moreover, from the day they are chosen, let a hand be laid on them and let them be exorcised daily. And when the day draws near on which they are to be baptised, let the bishop (himself) exorcise each one of them, that he may be certain that he is purified. But if there is one who is not purified let him be put on one side because he did not hear the word of instruction with faith. For the [evil and] strange spirit remained with him.[1]

These exorcisms, which later came to be known as the scrutinies, required a complex set of liturgical actions, including prayer, anointings, and renunciations of Satan intended to purify the candidate. These scrutinies were spiritual, having to do with the heart. They were not intended to examine a person's knowledge of the truth in intellectual terms. Instead, they addressed the heart and conscience, the soul and the will. They had to do with disposition, intention, purpose, and orientation. They related to the battle of the heart with lust, greed, envy, anger, hatred, and the like. They expressed the conflict that all God's people have with the lure of evil, with the temptation to pursue the world, the flesh, and the devil. Augustine defined the role of both the church and the candidates in these scrutinies. "We heap upon the head of your enemy all the anathemas which his heinous crimes deserve. On your part, give yourselves completely to this glorious battle, so that with proper horror you may renounce all your contacts with him."[2]

The daily exorcisms described by Hippolytus occurred on the six days of Holy Week before the baptism. They culminated in the bishop's exorcism and in the rite of breathing. According to Hippolytus, "Laying his hand on them he shall exorcise every evil spirit to flee away from them and never to return to them [henceforward]. And when he has finished exorcising, let him breathe on [their faces] and seal their foreheads and ears and noses and (then) let him raise them up."[3]

The tradition of breathing in the face of the candidate relates to the ancient understanding of the Holy Spirit. It rests on the belief that when God created Adam and "breathed into his nostrils the breath of life" (Gen. 2:7), it was the Holy Spirit that he received. When Adam and Eve fell away from God, they lost the presence of the Holy Spirit in their lives and in the lives of their descendents. But now, in conversion, the Holy Spirit is given back again. Consequently, the rite of exorcism and the rite of breathing are closely related. For as one rite rids the candidate of the spirit of evil, the other symbolizes the new infusion of the Holy Spirit. The rite of sealing the candidate with the sign of the cross on the forehead, ears, and nose complements the exorcisms and breathing, because it symbolizes the promise of salvation that comes from the unfailing love of God. Together, these three rites point to the meaning of baptism, for they symbolize the passage from the clutches of the evil one to the realm of God's kingdom, the church.

While the rite of exorcism symbolized the purification of the candidate, the presentations developed in the fourth century symbolized enlightenment and illumination. In special Lenten ceremonies, the candidate received the creed and the Lord's Prayer, which embody the church's tradition of faith and prayer. Like the scrutinies, the presentations are not to be seen as symbols of a mere intellectual Christianity. Rather, they are symbols of the weapons Christians have in their warfare against the power of evil.

In the ancient church, the creed was delivered orally and candidates were required to memorize it verbatim. Handing the creed down orally rather than in written form emphasized its living power in a person's life, as opposed to an objective, intellectual statement of faith that did not touch a person's life. In the mid-fourth century, Cyril of Jerusalem, who was well known for his catechetical lectures delivered in the church of the Holy Sepulchre, told the candidate to memorize the creed and to "keep this faith as the only provision you need for your journey all the rest of your life, and receive no other."[4] As this example shows, the creed is delivered to the candidate as food, sustenance, and nourishment. It feeds the soul, strengthens the heart, and aids the convert in the battle with the powers of evil. It defines the Christian's place in the world and permeates the whole of his or her actions. Augustine captured this spirit of the creed by telling new converts that "it will be written in your hearts, so that you may love what you believe and that, through love, faith may work in you and that you may become pleasing to the Lord God."[5]

The *Pilgrimage of Egira* describes the manner in which the presentation of the creed took place in Jerusalem. According to Egira, the instructor taught the creed during Lent, phrase by phrase, explaining both its literal and spiritual meaning. Then, at the end of Lent, the bishop's chair was placed behind the altar. When the bishop sat in his seat, the candidates for baptism came one by one and recited the creed from memory.[6]

Like the creed, the Lord's Prayer was also committed to memory. While the converting Christian had already been taught to pray, the Lord's Prayer was viewed as a prayer reserved for baptized Christians, in the spirit of Augustine: "How can someone say, 'Our Father' if he has not yet been born?"[7] The emphasis placed on this prayer by the early church fathers had to do not only with what the convert wanted from the Father, but what the candidate for baptism ought to have wanted. Specifically, what the candidate ought to have wanted was God's will to be done in his or her life, as God's will was done on earth.

Both of these rituals—the creed and the Lord's Prayer—

embody what theologian Michel Dujarier calls "the formulas which have carried the church's traditions of faith and of prayer from one generation of believers to the next."[8] Perhaps we can assume that when the candidates received the creed and the Lord's Prayer, they knew they were being entrusted with the heart of the gospel. They knew they were soon to be initiated into this truth and an approach to life that they had been converting to for several years.

APPLICATION TO CONTEMPORARY EVANGELISM

Although the twentieth century may seem worlds apart from the third and fourth centuries, the spirit of the contemporary age does not differ vastly from the pagan era of antiquity. In our time of secularization, materialism, sensualism, and violence, the need to be aware of the principalities and powers that pull us into the evils of the day is every bit as urgent as it has been in the past. Consequently, the period of purification and enlightenment in modern liturgical evangelism maintains the spirit of the early church. It is a time "to purify minds and hearts by the examination of conscience and by repentance, and also to enlighten those minds and hearts by a deeper knowledge of Christ the Savior."[9] For this reason both the scrutinies and the presentations have been adapted to the modern era.

As in the ancient church, the period of purification and enlightenment today is not intellectual. It is not a time to study doctrine, ethics, and scripture. Rather, it is a time for reflection, a time to enter the desert and be alone, a time to recall memories of the spiritual journey.

The image of the desert has always represented going to the heart of the conflict. The arid, lifeless desert conveys the power of evil to destroy God's creation, to spoil it, and to turn it into a wasteland. Here in the desert, God's people wrestle with the power of evil before moving on to proclaim God's power over evil. Moses, the prophets, John the Baptist, Jesus, Paul, and, after them, the hermits of the early church went to the desert. They went to the desert not to escape temptation, but to confront it and to overcome it. The spirit of Lent and the practice of purification and enlightenment during Lent by the converting persons is that of the desert. At this time, the faithful wrestle once more with the demons that would draw them toward evil, a process which is at the heart of conversion. They conquer those demons in the name of Jesus and adorn themselves with the weapons of the Holy Spirit. Both the scrutinies and the presentations assist this journey into the desert. They help the converting person to recollect his or her spiritual journey and assist him or her in moving more deeply into the life of the Holy Spirit.

The scrutinies in modern liturgical evangelism fulfill a twofold purpose. First, they recall what is "weak, defective, or sinful in the hearts of the elect, so that it may be healed," and second, they reveal "what is upright, strong, and holy, so that it may be strengthened."[10]

The scrutinies are conducted in the context of the Sunday morning service of worship, usually right after the sermon. They occur three times—on the third, fourth, and fifth Sundays in Lent. In each scrutiny the liturgy of the Word concentrates on the meaning of Christ the Redeemer. The first Sunday emphasizes Christ the living water (the story of the Samaritan woman); the second Sunday emphasizes Christ as the light (the story of the man born blind); and the final Sunday sets Jesus forth as the resurrection and the life (the story of the raising of Lazarus). Each of these accounts allows the minister to develop a homily that guides the candidate in the inner assessment of his or her own pilgrimage to conversion.

A period of silent prayer for the elect follows the homily. The elect are invited to stand together with their sponsors in the front of the church. The leader of worship invites the congregation to pray for the elect, to pray particularly that they may be characterized by a sense of sin, a spirit of repentance, and a knowledge of their acceptance by God. Then the elect are invited to pray and to express a spirit of repentance through some physical gesture.

Then there follows an audible prayer for the elect. During the prayer the sponsor places his hand on the shoulder of the candidate and the leader prays for special intentions such as that "they may keep the word of God in their hearts," that "they may learn to know Christ," that "they may sincerely reject anything in their lives which is displeasing to Christ or opposed to him."[11]

Finally, the exorcism takes place. The modern provisional text[12] suggests a threefold action. First, the celebrant, asking all the elect to join hands with him, prays to God on behalf of the group. The prayer consists of intercessions such as "never let the powers of evil deceive them" and "free them from the spirit of falsehood." Second, if time permits, hands are laid upon each individual with a particular brief prayer for that person. Third, the exorcism concludes with a prayer to Jesus, with hands extended over the elect. This prayer calls upon Jesus to work his love and salvation in them.

These scrutinies play an important role in bringing the inner experience of conversion to a climax. For in the scripture readings, the sermons, and the prayers, the whole spiritual journey of one or more years is reenacted in a brief yet significantly personal way. The intensity of these actions brings the meaning of conversion into focus once again and assists the converting person in the deepening of his or her commitment.

The same can be said for the presentations.[13] While converts today are more familiar with both the creed and the Lord's Prayer than they were in the third century, the dramatic effect of handing over the church's tradition of faith and prayer is no less effective. It is recommended that the presentation be made sometime after the scrutinies, perhaps in a weekday service. However, many prefer the presentation to be made in a Sunday service.

Imagine that you have gone through the entire process of conversion, that you are deeply committed to the faith and to prayer, and that you are now anxiously awaiting the day of your baptism. Here you are, perhaps on the last Sunday of Lent, now standing before the minister in the presence of the congregation you have come to love as your extended family. The minister says, My dear friends, listen carefully to the words of that faith by which you are to be justified. The words are few, but the mysteries they contain are awe-inspiring. Accept them with a sincere heart and be faithful to them." Then, following the lead of the minister, you recite from memory the Apostles' Creed, savoring every phrase, every word. For here is something more than a statement of faith, it is a credo of life, a commitment from which you view and live all of life. Then, in this or another service of worship, you are given the rule of prayer. Again, you are invited to say the Lord's Prayer, not just as words, but as the fundamental commitment of your life. With each phrase and word, you recall the instruction and values that you received and by which you now live.

These presentations are not mere formalities; they have to do with the very essence of that tradition that reaches back through history to the time of Christ and his apostles. What they believed and taught has been handed down from generation to generation in the church. Now, almost two thousand years after the event, the candidate accepts that tradition with the spiritual intent and meaning that countless millions of people throughout history have experienced. This is no dry, rote action. It trembles with an inexpressible mystery, immerses the elect in the meaning of faith, and penetrates into their very being.

The period of purification and enlightenment, of spiritual journey preceding baptism, emphasizes not instruction, but spiritual recollection and readiness. It brings before the converting person the essence of what it means to be converted to Christ and equips the new convert with the weapons of spiritual warfare. It calls the convert into an ultimate rejection of Satan and all works of evil. It bids the convert to receive the tradition of faith and prayer that has been handed down in the church from the beginnings of Christianity. Rejecting Satan and accepting the tradition is absolutely essential to conversion. The period of purification and enlightenment with its exorcisms and presentations provides the converting person with one more opportunity to deepen his or her commitment to Jesus Christ as Lord and Savior.

NOTES

1. *The Treatise on the Apostolic Tradition of St. Hippolytus of Rome*, 30-31.
2. Quoted by Michel Dujarier, *The Rites of Christian Initiation* (New York: Sadlier, 1979), p. 121.
3. *The Treatise on the Apostolic Tradition of St. Hippolytus of Rome*, 32.
4. Quoted by Dujarier, *Rites*, p. 139.
5. Ibid., 140.
6. Ibid., 139

7. Ibid., 141
8. Ibid., 134
9. U.S. Catholic Conference, *RCIA.* 6.
10. U. S. Catholic Conference, *Rite.* 6.
11. For the text of these prayers, see U.S. Catholic Conference, *RCIA.* para. 163. For the full text of the three scrutinies, see *RCIA.* para. 160–180.
12. U.S. Catholic Conference, *RCIA.* para. 164.
13. For the full text of the presentations, see U.S. Catholic Conference, *RCIA.* para. 183–192.

7. The Rite of Initiation

The converting process culminates in the rite of initiation. Baptism symbolizes the forgiveness of sin, chrismation represents admittance into the people of God, and receiving the Eucharist symbolizes sharing in the life of the Holy Spirit.

I grew up in the home of a Baptist pastor, where adult baptism was the norm. Nevertheless, as an infant I was dedicated in the arms of my parents. While this dedication differed from infant baptism in that water was not used, it was similar to infant baptism in that it called upon God to choose me as his own and it placed upon my parents and the congregation the duty of bringing me up in the faith.

I was baptized as a teenager. Although it was a simple baptism, it contained some basic symbols that I have never forgotten. For example, baptism was treated as a necessary aspect of my converting process. Baptism was not an option, something that could be done or not, depending on my whim or fancy. I was aware that if I refused to be baptized, I would in effect be rejecting the faith. On the other hand, I recognized that my choice to be baptized was a sign of my acceptance of the faith. I saw baptism as my public witness to faith. It was an action that spoke louder than words. It was my physical yes to Christ and his church.

Several simple symbols that surrounded my baptism have their roots in the ancient baptism of the church. The primary symbol was immersion in water in the name of Jesus Christ. This action symbolized my burial with Christ and my resurrection with him from the tomb. Three other symbols, which were secondary but still of great importance, were the robing, the renunciation, and the affirmation. I was dressed in white robes to signify my new relationship to Christ. Then, in the water I was asked, "Do you renounce Satan and all his works?" To which I answered, "I do." And, finally, after the renunciation I was asked, "Do you receive Jesus Christ as your Lord and Savior?" To which I answered, "I do." I was unaware that these three symbols originated in the primitive Christian community. But I did sense the powerful meaning they contained. Consequently, the baptismal ceremony, simple as it was, made a lasting impression upon me. To this day when I am asked to give testimony to my faith, I always go back to my baptism as the turning point of my personal experience with Christ.

BIBLICAL BACKGROUND

The New Testament contains a considerable number of stories and allusions to baptism that reveal the roots of the meaning of baptism and the origins of later symbolic ceremonies. By exploring these texts for the meaning of baptism and by identifying the symbols that surrounded baptism in the New Testament, we will discover the roots of the rite of initiation.[1] Baptism in the primitive Christian community clearly had a twofold meaning: it identified the convert with the death and resurrection of Christ and brought the convert into a new relationship with the church. For example, the convert was seen as the recipient of the work of Jesus. The convert was "baptized into his death" in order to "walk in newness of life." The impact of baptism was "that our old self was crucified with him so that the sinful body might be destroyed, and we might no longer be enslaved to sin" (Rom. 6:1–10). Here baptism is seen as a turning point, the event that marks the convert's turning away from the powers of evil toward the kingdom of Christ. But this is only made possible because of what Christ has done. He has defeated the powers of sin and death in his own death and resurrection. This victory is then passed on to the convert through baptism. Thus baptism realizes the saving effect of Jesus' work.

The other broad meaning of baptism is that it brings the convert into a new community of people, the church. Baptism is never portrayed in the New Testament as individualistic salvation. It is always salvation into a new society of people, the body of Christ. In the description of the earliest Christian conversions, the converts were "added" to the church (Acts 2:41). This implies that they did not start a new church, but were included in the one church, the one body of Christ that had already been formed. Consequently, thirty years later Paul wrote to the Corinthians reminding them that "by one Spirit we are all baptized into one body—Jews or Greeks, slaves or free—and all were made to drink of one Spirit" (1 Cor. 12:13).

From these two meanings of baptism—sharing in the Christ event and entering the community of faith—the New Testament church developed a number of symbols to convey in action as well as in words the meaning of baptism. Those New Testament sources may be organized into three categories: (1) rites that developed around the meaning of baptism, (2) rites that reflect biblical images of baptism, and (3) rites that relate to the reception of the Holy Spirit.

First, we have inherited many rites that relate to the meaning of baptism. For example, baptism begins with the apostolic proclamation of salvation through Christ, symbolized in the third century by the inquiry. However, while the kerygma may have been sufficient in the early Hebraic context, the situation of the Hellenists made it necessary to have more content. Specifically, two matters were added: Paul speaks of the necessity of believing in one God (1 Thess. 1:9), which may account for the development of the study of the creed during the catechumenate. Second, Paul refers to the standard of teaching (Rom. 6:17), which accounts for the development of the baptismal catechesis, stressing way of life (see Gal. 5:16–25). While the Jewish converts who already believed in one God and had the law were in less need of this instruction, the Gentiles who were polytheistic and amoral were in great need of instruction in faith and morals. This need probably stands behind the development of the catechumenate.

The meaning of baptism is also conveyed by the action of putting off the old life and putting on the new life in Christ. For example, the major rites of transition, such as the rite of welcome, the rite of election, and the rites of initiation, relate to the New Testament idea of "putting on" Christ. Some lesser rites, such as disrobing before baptism and putting on the new white robe after baptism also relate to this idea. These symbols capture the essence of Paul's instruction that in conversion and baptism we "put off" the old man and "put on" the new man (Col. 3:1–17). The idea of transference from one kingdom to another can also be traced to the baptismal hymns of the New Testament, which celebrate crossing over into the kingdom of Christ.[2] Finally, the most essential aspect of baptism, the immersion in water in the name of the Father, Son, and Holy Spirit, also conveys the concept of transition, for it symbolizes burial into Christ's death and a rising to new spiritual life through his resurrection.

Second, other symbols and ceremonies in the rite of initiation may be traced back to certain biblical typologies. For example, baptism is compared to the crossing of the Red Sea by the Israelites (1 Cor. 10:1–2). The manna/Eucharist typology is employed in John, chapter 6. Next, circumcision is seen as a stripping away of the old flesh (Col. 2:11–12). And finally, a number of allusions refer to the new birth (Titus 3:5; 1 Peter 1:3; 2:2; John 2:3–5). These images not only provide the source for later ceremonial developments in the rite of initiation, but also seem to imply that ceremonial actions already accompanied baptism in the New Testament community.

Third, baptism is related to the reception of the Holy Spirit in the New Testament. Paul associates baptism and the reception of the Spirit. "You were washed, you were sanctified, you were justified in the name of the Lord Jesus Christ and in the Spirit of our God." (1 Cor. 1:21–22). In several specific instances, the laying on of hands was an accompanying rite (Acts 8; Acts 9; Heb. 6:2). The laying on of hands is a rich gesture that symbolizes the gift of the Holy Spirit. Surely this lies behind the later rite of anointing with oil after the baptism to symbolize the gift of the Holy Spirit in the life of the new believer.

Both the meaning and practice of baptism in the New Testament take place on a trajectory. The development of baptism does not end with the close of the first century, but continues in the second and third century. But it develops in keeping with its primitive meaning and roots, enriched by actions that convey the meaning of conversion into Christ and the church.

THE EXPERIENCE OF THE EARLY CHURCH

The meaning of baptism and the symbolic actions that convey that meaning coalesce in the third-century rite of initiation. While the fully developed rites are described for us in *The Apostolic Tradition* of Hippolytus, the basic structure of these rites is already referred to by Justin Martyr in the mid-second century. According to Justin, the rite of baptism has three parts: (1) preparation of the community before Easter, (2) the baptism itself, and (3) the final eucharistic celebration with the whole community.[3] For a more fully developed insight into these three parts, we turn to *The Apostolic Tradition* of Hippolytus.

First, the baptismal candidates were prepared before Easter.

> Those who are to receive baptism shall fast on the Friday and on the Saturday. And on the Saturday the bishop shall assemble those who are to be baptised in one place, and shall bid them [all] to pray and bow the knee. And laying his hand on them he shall exorcise every evil spirit to flee away from them and never to return to them [henceforward]. And when he has finished exorcising, let him breathe on [their faces] and seal their foreheads and ears and noses and [then] let him raise them up. And they shall spend all the night in vigil, reading the scriptures [to them] and instructing them.[4]

Today, Easter consists of a number of liturgical celebrations. Most churches have services on Maundy Thursday, Good Friday, Saturday night, and Easter. However, in the third century, the Easter celebration was a single event, conducted on Saturday night only. The candidates for baptism were to fast starting on Friday. Then on Saturday a final exorcism was followed by the rite of Ephpheta, the sealing of the senses. Next, the candidates came to the vigil and listened to readings and instruction concerning baptism and the new life in Christ.

Second, the rite of baptism centered around immersion in water.

> And at the hour when the cock crows they shall first (of all) pray over the water. [When they come to the water, let the water be pure and flowing.] And they shall put off their clothes. And

they shall baptise the little children first. And if they can answer for themselves, let them answer. But if they cannot, let their parents answer or someone from their family. And next they shall baptise the grown men; and last the women, who shall [all] have loosed their hair and laid aside the gold ornaments [which they were wearing]. Let no one go down to the water having any alien object with [them].[5]

From the very beginnings of Christian baptism, water has been one of the major symbols of new birth. While water does symbolize washing and cleansing, the central symbolic power of water is its power to create. The fathers of the church point out that the earth was formed out of the waters, that the waters were the first to receive the command to bring forth living creatures, and that our own human gestation takes place in water.[6] Stripping off old clothes, entering the waters naked, and then being clothed in a new white garment emphasized the complete rebirth of baptism. (In the third century, because of the common baths, nudity did not mean what it does today.)

The next step in the baptism was the final renunciation.

And at the time determined for baptising the bishop shall give thanks over the oil and put it into a vessel and [it is called] the Oil of Thanksgiving.

And he shall take [also] other oil and exorcise over it, and it is called Oil of Exorcism. And let a deacon carry the Oil of Exorcism and stand on the left hand [of the presbyter] (who will do the anointing). And another deacon shall take the Oil of Thanksgiving and stand on the right hand. And when the presbyter takes hold of each one of those who are to be baptised, let him bid him renounce saying: I renounce thee, Satan, and all thy service and all thy works.

And when he has said this let him anoint him with the Oil of Exorcism saying: Let all evil spirits depart far from thee.[7]

While the renunciation of Satan was traditional in all the churches, a great deal of variety in the ceremony existed. In some churches the renunciation occurred as the candidate faced the West, the direction of Satan's kingdom. He then took off his outer garment, stood on a piece of animal hide to symbolize the skins worn by Adam and Eve, and with outstretched arms renounced Satan. This action was followed by the allegiance to the triune God.

In the writings of Hippolytus, the allegiance, the creed, and the baptism in the name of the Father, Son, and Holy Spirit are prescribed in the following manner:

> Then after these things let him give him over to [the presbyter] who stands at the water [to baptise]: And a presbyter takes his right hand and then he turns his face to the East. Before he descends into the water, while he still turns his face to the East, standing above the water he says after receiving the Oil of Exorcism, thus: I believe and bow me unto Thee and all Thy service, O Father, Son and Holy Ghost. And so he descends into the water. And let them stand in the water naked. And let [a] deacon likewise go down with him into the water. And let him say to him and instruct him: Dost thou believe in one God the Father Almighty and His only-begotten Son Jesus Christ our Lord and our Saviour, and His Holy Spirit, Giver of life to all creatures, the Trinity of one Substance, one God-head, one Lordship, one Kingdom, one Faith, one Baptism in the Holy Catholic Apostolic Church for life eternal [Amen]? And he who is baptised shall say [again] thus: Verily, I believe.
>
> And [when] he [who is to be baptised] goes down to the water, let him who baptises lay a hand on him saying thus:
> Dost thou believe in God the Father Almighty?
> And he who is being baptised shall say:
> I believe.
> Let him forthwith baptise him once, having his hand laid upon his head.
> And after (this) let him say:
> Dost thou believe in Christ Jesus, the Son of God,
> Who was born of the Holy Spirit and the Virgin Mary,
> Who was crucified in the days of Pontius Pilate,
> And died, [and was buried]
> And rose the third day living from the dead
> And ascended into [the] heaven[s],
> And sat down to judge the living and the dead?
> And when he says: I believe, let him [baptise him] the second time.
> And again let him say:
> Dost thou believe in (the) Holy Spirit, in the Holy Church,
> And the resurrection of the flesh?
> And he who is being baptised shall say: I believe.
> And so let him [baptise him] the third time.[8]

The creed found in Hippolytus is the forerunner of the Apostles' Creed known as the interrogatory creed. It asks for allegiance to the faith of the church handed down from apostolic times. In this context it is not a mere intellectual assent to particular propositions of faith, but a pact with Christ that replaces the pact with the devil.

After the baptism into the triune God, the baptism continued with the chrismation, the sealing of the Spirit.

And afterwards when he comes up [from the water] he shall be anointed by the presbyter with the Oil of Thanksgiving saying:
I anoint thee with holy oil in the Name of Jesus Christ.
And [so] each one drying himself [with a towel] they shall [now] put on their clothes, [and after this let them be together in the assembly].
And the Bishop shall lay his hand upon them invoking and saying:
O Lord God, who didst count these [Thy servants] worthy [of deserving] the forgiveness of sins by the laver of regeneration, [make them worthy to be filled with] Thy Holy Spirit and send upon them Thy grace, that they may serve Thee according to Thy will; [for] to Thee (is) the glory, to the Father and to the Son with (the) Holy Ghost in the holy Church; both now [and ever] and world without end. Amen.
After this pouring [the consecrated] oil [from his hand] and laying [his hand] on his head, he shall say:
I anoint thee with holy oil in God the Father Almighty and Christ Jesus and the Holy Ghost.
And sealing [him] on the forehead, he shall give him the kiss [of peace] and say:
The Lord be with you.
And he who has been sealed shall say:
And with thy spirit.[9]

The sealing of the Spirit is in keeping with the conviction that all baptized believers have the indwelling Spirit, the seal of God's promise of salvation. This sealing is done in the spirit of Paul: "In him you also, who have heard the word of truth, the gospel of your salvation, and have believed in him, were sealed with the promised Holy Spirit" (Eph. 1:13).

Next, the newly baptized candidates, now members of

the church, were brought into full fellowship with the Christian community. Now for the first time they were permitted to pray with the faithful and to give the kiss of peace.

> Thenceforward they shall pray together with all the people. But they shall not previously pray with the faithful before they have undergone all these things. And after the prayers, let them give the kiss of peace.[10]

Finally, in the third part of the rite of initiation, the newly baptized were invited to participate for the first time in the Eucharist. Imagine how high the feelings must have run. For more than three years, the candidate had been in the process of converting to Christ. On Easter morning, after a long, perhaps arduous, yet meaningful journey into the waters of baptism, the candidate was finally privileged to feast at the table of the Lord.

> And then let the oblation [at once] be brought by the deacons to the bishop, and he shall eucharistize [first] the bread into the representation, [which the Greek calls the antitype] of the Flesh of Christ; [and] the cup mixed with wine for the antitype, [which the Greek calls the likeness] of the Blood which was shed for all who have believed in him; and milk and honey mingled together in fulfillment of the promise which was (made) to the Fathers, wherein He said I will give you a land flowing with milk and honey; which Christ indeed gave, (even) His Flesh, whereby they who believe are nourished like little children, making the bitterness of the (human) heart sweet by the sweetness of His word. Water also for an oblation for a sign of the laver, that the inner man also, which is psychic, may receive the same (rites) as the body. And the bishop shall give an explanation concerning all these things to them who receive.
> And when he breaks the Bread in distributing to each a fragment he shall say:
> The Bread of Heaven in Christ Jesus.
> And he who receives shall answer: Amen.
> And the Presbyters—but if there are not enough (of them) the deacons also—shall hold the cups and stand by in good order and with reverence: first he that holdeth the water, second he who holds the milk, third he who holds the wine.

And they who partake shall taste of each (cup), he who gives (it)
saying thrice:
> In God the Father Almighty;
and he who receives shall say: Amen.
> And in the Lord Jesus Christ;
(and he shall say: Amen.)
> And in (the) Holy Spirit [and] in the Holy Church;
and he shall say: Amen. So shall it be done to each one."

The milk and honey symbolize the hope of Israel for the
promised land. Here, in the Christian sense, they symbolize
entrance into the church, the promises of salvation, the new
birth, and the sweetness of Christ.

The rite of initiation as described by Hippolytus is clearly
modeled on the meaning and the symbols of baptism in the
New Testament. It culminates a process that brings a person
into a saving relationship with Jesus Christ. It is not a mere
formality, but a genuine path toward a relationship that will
be nurtured in the church.

APPLICATION TO CONTEMPORARY EVANGELISM

Like the ancient practice of baptism, the modern rites of
initiation culminate the process of salvation. From the very
beginning, external rites have helped to form the internal
reality of Christian conversion. Externally, these final services bring a person into the full fellowship of the church,
and internally, they enable the candidate to reenact the entire
process of conversion. On one hand, the death and resurrection of Christ is reenacted. On the other hand, the convert's
personal and subjective experience of being born anew is
also reenacted. The rites of initiation therefore represent the
whole process of conversion through representation.

The calendar setting for initiation into Christ and the

church has a crucial symbolic importance. In the ancient church and now in modern liturgical evangelism, initiation takes place in the context of the Easter celebration. At Easter the candidate's rebirth coincides with the mystery of Christ's death and resurrection. In the ancient church, Easter was celebrated in a single event stretched over three days called the *triduum.* Christians fasted on Friday and Saturday and feasted on Sunday. On Saturday the candidates for baptism underwent the preparatory rites. Then the whole congregation gathered at dusk and remained in worship until dawn. At dawn the candidates were baptized, chrismated, and, together with the entire Christian community, received the bread and wine, the symbols of their Savior's death and resurrection.

Today the elements of the ancient Saturday night vigil are abbreviated into a two or three hour service. As in the ancient church, the service of initiation contains four parts: the preparation, baptism, chrismation (or confirmation), and receiving the Eucharist. An examination of the structure and meaning of each of these parts will help us grasp the spiritual significance of the service of initiation.[12]

The preparation for baptism includes four parts:

—Recitation of the profession of faith
—Rite of Ephpheta or opening of ears and mouth
—Choosing of a Christian name
—Anointing with the oil of catechumens.

Because of the length of the Saturday night service, the preparation is done by many churches on Holy Saturday or before. For all Christians Holy Saturday is a solemn day set aside for prayer, repentance, and meditation on the death of Christ. For this reason the candidates spend the day in prayerful recollection of their conversion journey. The celebration of the rites of preparation assists the candidates in focusing on the meaning of their spiritual journey and provides them with some external rites that express this inner journey. The rite of Ephpheta and the anointing with oil emphasize God's action in the saving journey, while the creed and the choosing of a Christian name signify the candidate's response to God's choosing.

The second phase of the rite of initiation is the baptism itself. The baptism contains the following parts:

—Final words of instruction by the minister
—A prayer litany remembering the saints of the church
—A prayer of blessing over the waters
—The final renunciation of Satan
—An anointing with oil
—The rite of baptism
—Clothing with the white garment
—Presentation of the lighted candle.

These parts as a whole symbolize salvation. For example, the instruction, the litany, the prayer over the waters, and the renunciation of Satan underscore the supernatural conflict between the powers of evil and Christ. The instruction and litany emphasize the mercifulness of God, who delivers his people from sin and evil. The blessing over the waters signifies God's grace. For through the waters, he saved Noah, brought forth Israel, baptized his son, and now creates anew these candidates. And now, in this final renunciation, the powers of heaven symbolized in the victory of Christ over sin confront the influence of Satan over the converting candidate. And the anointing with oil confirms that this person is indeed chosen of God and blessed by his salvation.

The dialectical action between God's saving work and human response culminates in the water baptism that professes faith in the triune God. Here in this action the promise of God to save is symbolized not only in the water, but in the immersion into the water and the raising from the water, which signify baptism into Christ's death and resurrection, the saving event of the world. When the newly baptized convert dons white garments, entrance into a new life in God's community, the church, is symbolized. And finally, when the new Christian is handed the lit candle, he or she is charged with being a child of the light in the world.

In these brief baptismal rites, the drama of salvation is told not only in words but actions. This story of salvation contains an exposition of the human condition, the conflict between the powers, and resolve. Now, because the alienation from God has been resolved, the new convert is ready for his or her chrismation. Chrismation, the third phase of initiation, is simple and direct. The minister addresses the newly baptized as "members of Christ and his priestly people" and tells them that they are now to receive the Holy Spirit. After a prayer the minister lays hands upon each of the newly baptized, and dipping his right thumb in the oil of chrism, he makes the sign of the cross on the forehead and seals the convert with the Holy Spirit. Finally, the new converts join in the glorious Easter celebration of the Eucharist. For the first time they feed upon the bread and drink the wine and thus enter into the mystery of participation in Christ.

As we have seen, the church has always recognized that baptism brings to the believing person the benefits of Christ's victory over the powers of evil. Consequently, from New Testament times, symbols and ceremonies have been developed to embody the convert's transition from the kingdom of Satan to the kingdom of Christ. The primary symbols of this conversion are baptism into the death and resurrection of Christ, reception of the Holy Spirit by chrismation, which signifies the new life in Christ, and receiving the Eucharist, which celebrates this mystery in the church.

NOTES

1. For a more detailed study, see Reginald H. Fuller, "Christian Initiation in the New Testament," in *Made, Not Born: New Perspectives on Christian Initiation and the Catechumenate,* Murphy Center for Liturgical Research (Notre Dame, Ind.: University of Notre Dame Press, 1976), 7–26.
2. See Gal. 3:28; Col. 1:12–14; Eph. 5:14; 1 Peter 2:10.
3. Justin Martyr, *First Apology,* 61, 65–66.
4. *The Treatise on the Apostolic Tradition of St. Hippolytus of Rome,* 32.
5. Ibid., 33.
6. See Tertullian, *On Baptism,* chap. 3
7. *The Treatise of the Apostolic Tradition of St. Hippolytus of Rome,* 34.
8. Ibid., 35-37.
9. Ibid., 37-39.
10. Ibid., 39.
11. Ibid., 40-42.
12. For the full text of the rites of initiation, see U.S. Catholic Conference, *Rite,* 193-234.

8. Mystagogia

During this period of postbaptismal instruction, the newly born spiritual infant is integrated into the life of the church.

Like everyone else, I have learned about my birth and infancy from my parents. They have described the little town in Pennsylvania where I was born, the aged family doctor, the rickety home hospital, the comments of the young nurse, and their own initial reactions to their newborn son. While I have no recollection of that event, I do know that I was loved, cared for, nursed, and coddled from the day I was born. That parental love and tender care saw me through my infancy and brought me into childhood. Without that parental aid and concern, I may not have grown into a responsible member of the family.

Mystagogia, which means "learning the mysteries," is the period of spiritual infancy. During this time the newborn infant is nursed and cared for, so that its entry into the Christian family is pleasant and fruitful. Mystagogia emphasizes teaching the mysteries of the faith, especially those concerning the sacraments. For these mysteries are the means by which the newborns are nursed and nourished in their new life.

THE BIBLICAL BACKGROUND

There is no such thing as an institution of mystagogia in the New Testament. However, the tender love and concern for the infant convert, which is the purpose of mystagogia, is clearly indicated in a number of texts.

First, the New Testament recognizes the new convert as an infant in the faith. For example, Peter refers to his reader as "newborn babes" and admonishes them to "long for the pure spiritual milk, that by it you may grow up to salvation" (1 Pet. 2:2). This concern for the growth of the spiritual infant is also captured by the writer of Hebrews, who urged his readers to "go on to maturity" (Heb. 5:1).

Furthermore, the New Testament text implies that new converts were given special spiritual attention. They were looked upon as newborn infants in need of spiritual nourishment. For example, Luke, after describing the conversion of more than three thousand persons at Pentecost, reports that when they were brought into the body of Christ, "they devoted themselves to the Apostles' teaching and fellowship, to the breaking of bread and prayers" (Acts 2:42). Luke is describing instruction, worship, spirituality, and fellowship —four of the major nutrients for a spiritually healthy infant.

Finally, the New Testament contains several examples of converts who were nourished in the church. According to Luke, Paul spent some time with the disciples at Damascus after his conversion. The text states, "For several days he was with the disciples." Immediately thereafter Luke reports that Paul proclaimed Jesus as "the Son of God" (Acts 9:20). While we don't know the subject of instruction, Paul's sermon in Acts 9:20 seems to suggest the disciples spent some time nurturing Paul in the basic mysteries of the incarnation, death, and resurrection of Jesus.

In 2 Timothy Paul speaks of the nurturing quality demonstrated by Timothy's grandmother and mother. "I am reminded of your sincere faith, a faith that dwelt first in your grandmother Lois and your mother Eunice, and now, I am sure dwells in you" (2 Tim 1:5). We also know of Paul's interest and concern for Timothy, a nurturing quality that led Paul to refer to Timothy as "my beloved child" (1 Tim 1:2).

These texts and examples illustrate what lies at the heart of the period of mystagogia. It is a time to integrate these new converts into the household of faith. They are babes in Christ, infants who need to be reassured, children who need to be received into the family of God's people, the church.

THE EXPERIENCE OF THE EARLY CHURCH

There is abundant evidence in the early church that new-born Christians were not left without spiritual direction after baptism. In the first three centuries, Christian churches were quite small. Those who were converted were integrated into a supportive community from which they received personal support and direction. Hippolytus's account of the period immediately after baptism supports this view.

And when these things have been accomplished, let each one be zealous to perform good works and to please God, living righteously, devoting himself to the Church, performing the things which he has learnt, advancing in the service of God. And we have delivered to you briefly these things concerning Baptism and the Oblation because you have already been instructed concerning the resurrection of the flesh and the rest according to the Scriptures. But if there is any other matter which ought to be told, let the bishop impart it secretly to those who are communicated. He shall not tell this to any but the faithful and only after they have first been communicated. This is the white stone of which John said that there is a new name written upon it which no man knows except him who receives [the stone].[1]

This text reveals two concerns of the third-century church in Rome for its new converts. First, they were expected to lead a life in keeping with their Christian commitment.

While we have no information on this expectation, we are safe in assuming that the more mature Christian was expected to be the model for this life-style. Perhaps this role was played by the sponsor. Second, the text reveals concern that additional instruction be given to the convert after baptism. This is indicated in the mystery surrounding the white stone. However, the identification of the white stone is not known. Some scholars think it may refer to the Lord's Prayer, since Hippolytus does not mention the prayer previously in the text.[2]

The meaning of this postbaptismal catechesis may be derived from references in the writings of various church fathers from the second and third centuries. In the mid-second century, Justin Martyr indicates that the newborn Christians were immediately made to feel like members of the family. "We lead him to where those whom are called our brothers are assembled. We pray together fervently . . . then we give each other the kiss of peace."[3] Tertullian tells the candidates for baptism that after baptism they will "join hands with another and with brothers."[4]

Clement of Alexandria, in a treatise entitled *To the Newly Baptized,* offers the following instruction:

> May all actions and all words be turned toward God. Bring all your concerns to Christ, and at every instant, turn your soul toward God. Base all your reflections solidly on the power of Christ, so that it may rest calmly, sheltered from the waves of all needless talk and agitation, in the divine light of the savior. Day after day, share your thinking with men, but join it to that of God, during the day as well as at night. Do not let yourself fall into a deep sleep which closes your eyes and deadens your mind to prayers and hymns, for this kind of sleep is a prelude to death. Keep yourself always in active union with Christ who sends you from heaven his brilliant light. May Christ be your constant and unending joy.[5]

The vision Clement sets forth for the new Christian is a spirituality of growth. Baptism, rather than ending the spiritual pilgrimage, sets in motion a new phase of the journey, from baptism to the end of one's life. Consequently, all of life is to be lived in the baptismal waters. The meaning of baptism is a constant and unending source for the Christian life. It must permeate the Christian life so that the convert does not depart from it even in the thought patterns of sleep.

The early church also had specific postbaptismal rites. These rites assisted the new converts in achieving a spiritual recollection of their baptism and stimulated them toward further growth. The most widespread postbaptismal symbol was the wearing of the white garment. The wearing of white garments has its biblical origins in the Pauline metaphor of the new convert clothed in Christ (Gal. 3:27) and in John's assertion that the redeemed stand "before the throne and before the Lamb, clothed in white robes" (Rev. 7:9, 13–14).

Cyril of Jerusalem captured the meaning of the white robes in the lectures he gave in Jerusalem in the fourth century.

Now that you have divested yourself of your former clothes and have clothed yourselves in spiritual white ones, you must always be clothed in white. By no means do we want you to understand by this that your clothes must always be white; but that you must be clothed with true whiteness and with spiritual splendor, so that you may say with blessed Isaiah: "My soul rejoices in the Lord, for he has clothed me with the garment of salvation and has wrapped me in a tunic of joy."[6]

The white garments were worn for a full week after Easter. During this week church members traditionally attended a daily Eucharist and heard sermons on the meaning of this and other sacraments. According to Egira, the mysteries in Jeru-

salem were unveiled so well that "no one can remain un-
moved by what they hear. . . . The people shout out loud
their approval so that even outside the church the cries of the
faithful can be heard."[7]

Evidence also indicates that considerable attention was
given to moral instruction in the postbaptismal period. For
example, John Chrysostom stressed the ongoing battle with
the powers of Satan and the need to be vigilant against the
powers of evil. He instructed his hearers that though "you
have indeed been baptized . . . if you are not led by the Spirit
of God, you will have lost the dignity which has been con-
ferred upon you."[8] The historical evidence demonstrates
that the newly evangelized and now baptized convert in the
early church was not left without spiritual supervision after
baptism. A definite period of continued teaching and
spiritual direction was provided, even though it was short in
duration.

APPLICATION TO CONTEMPORARY EVANGELISM

In modern liturgical evangelism the period of mystagogia
extends over the fifty days of Easter and includes occasional
celebrations during the year. Mystagogia is dominated by
three concerns, related to the Eucharist, the church, and the
world.

First, the provisional text of the RCIA speaks of the mystagogia as a time for converts to "understand the paschal
mystery more fully and bring it into their lives."[9] One must
keep in mind that the convert during the conversion journey
has only heard of the eucharistic celebration or seen it from
afar. Now, having been baptized, the convert enjoys the
spiritually refreshing privilege of celebrating at the Lord's
table on a regular basis.

The experience of tasting the death and resurrection of Jesus at the table of the Lord is a new stage in the convert's spiritual journey. It is a spiritual privilege gained, a new source of spiritual sustenance. For in the symbolic presentation of the death and resurrection of Christ, the heart of the Christian gospel is proclaimed. Consequently, the earnest believer will experience a continual renewal of his or her relationship with God through Christ at the table of the Lord. In addition, when that relationship is broken or in need of repair, the new convert may experience a spiritual healing of inner trouble and turmoil at the Eucharist.

If one applies the axiom "you cannot understand what you have not experienced" to mystagogia, it becomes apparent that the experience of God's saving and sustaining presence at the table of the Lord needs to be explored with the new convert. Because bread and wine are ultimately mysteries of God's saving action that cannot be explained, mystagogia does not define or intellectually exhaust the mystery. Rather, mystagogia allows the convert to share his or her experience at the table of the Lord and to grow in a deeper experience of God's loving grace.

Second, mystagogia is a time to deal with the mystery of the convert's relationship to the church. Although the new convert has been participating in the life of the church since the rite of welcome, baptism brings the convert into a new relationship with the church. Mystagogia must help the convert discern his or her gifts that may be put to work in the life of the church. The convert's sponsor may be especially helpful in this task.

Everyone has some kind of gift that can be offered to the church. It may be a natural gift of friendliness, an ability to make others feel welcome, a knack for drawing others into the life of church. Some are gifted teachers, readers, singers, actors, or artists whose talent can be used in the church. Others have acquired gifts from their vocations, such as the gift for administration or skills in maintenance. And always some converts feel called to become sponsors themselves and work toward the evangelization of others. Whatever the gift, it is crucial to identify those who long to put their talents to use in the community of faith. The need to be integrated into the life of the church at this point is strong. The opportunity ought not to be lost.

Third, mystagogia heightens the new convert's concern for the world. Christ gave himself for the salvation of the world. The church at worship and work is the sign of this redemption. Consequently, the church cannot be an entity unto itself in the world. What the soul is to the body, the church is to the world.

The church not only prays for the world, but also acts on behalf of the world. It opposes the evil powers that rage in the world not by words alone, but by actions. Mystagogia involves new converts in action as well as in prayer for the needs of the world. Concern for the poor and needy, the oppressed, the old, the uneducated, the rights of the unborn, the environment, nuclear war, and so on can be acted on by the new Christian.

In modern liturgical evangelism, this threefold integration into the church takes place in several ways. The Sunday morning service of worship deepens the new convert's faith and relationship to the church. Close attention to the scriptural readings and the sermons not only during mystagogia, but throughout the year provide a continued source of spiritual nourishment. The habit of regular involvement in the life of the church needs to be stressed immediately. In some churches the new converts wear white robes and sit together in Sunday services during the mystagogia. This not only accents the importance of this period for them but makes the entire congregation conscious of their integration and aware of the evangelistic mission of the church.

In addition to the Sunday service, many churches conduct a mystagogia retreat that allows converts to recollect the mystery of their journey into faith and make commitments toward the future. The new convert now has a story, a story of evangelization, catechesis, illumination, and entrance into the full life of the church. The retreat allows time to review the story and share it with others.

Finally, in most churches mystagogia concludes with a service, a final ritual which brings together the full journey, completes, and frees the newborn candidate to pursue new dimensions of their spiritual journey as full members of the church. Simple as this ritual may be, its importance cannot be overemphasized because it brings closure to the evangelizing phase of the journey.[10]

Mystagogia is, in evangelical terms, the follow-up. It solidifies conversion *within* the church, emphasizing that life in Christ is not a lonesome journey that one takes alone, but a journey in the context of community. Its biblical roots are captured in the concept of the newly born spiritual infant. Its historical image is best pictured by the white-robed throng gathered at the daily Eucharist. In the contemporary setting, these new Christians are integrated into the Eucharist, their offering of praise and thanksgiving to the Father. They are brought into the inner life of the church so that they may learn full participation in the body of Christ. And they commit themselves to a caring and responsible relationship to the world.

108 / *Liturgical Evangelism*

NOTES

1. *The Treatise on the Apostolic Tradition of St. Hippolytus of Rome,* 42-43.
2. Ibid.
3. Justin Martyr, *First Apology.* 65.
4. Tertullian, *On Baptism.* 20, 5.
5. Quoted from Michel Dujarier, *Rites of Christian Initiation.* 211.
6. Quoted by Dujarier, Ibid., 214
7. Quoted by Dujarier, Ibid., 213
8. Quoted by Dujarier, Ibid., 215
9. U.S. Catholic Conference, *RCIA.* 38.
10. The *Rite* does not provide a suggested ritual for the conclusion of mystagogia. For a sample service see Sandra De Gidio, O.S.M, *RCIA: The Rites Revisited.* 136–139.

Epilogue

Liturgical Evangelism is not meant to be read and laid aside as an illustration of evangelism in the early church. Rather, I hope that the local churches will find in the evangelism of the third century a viable model for evangelism today. For these churches two final words of instruction are in order.

First, the practice of liturgical evangelism requires discernable periods and rituals to mark the progress of time—the context of the church year. The church year is the most appropriate context for liturgical evangelism because it is an extension of worship itself. While every Sunday service essentially celebrates the birth, death, resurrection, ascension, and second coming of Jesus Christ, the church year extends the celebration of these events over a full year. Consequently, when the various periods and stages of liturgical evangelism coincide with the events of the church year, a deeper, more profound sense of the mystery of Christ and the salvation he brings is realized by the converting person.

The cycle of evangelism through worship best begins with Pentecost Sunday. On this Sunday, in keeping with its meaning, the church members who have been called to evangelism are commissioned in a special ceremony. During the summer they evangelize friends and neighbors. In the fall they bring the converting person to the inquiry, acting as sponsor. Sometime in the fall, before Advent, the rite of entrance takes place. Then, during Advent and Epiphany the new convert enters the period of the catechumenate. (Many churches feel this is too short a time for the catechumenate. They therefore extend the catechumenate for more than a year, conducting catechesis from Advent through Epiphany of the following year.)

The rite of election then occurs on the first Sunday of Lent. During Lent the intense spiritual preparation of purification and enlightenment takes place. On the Saturday night Easter vigil, the candidates are baptized. Finally, during the fifty days of Easter season, mystagogia takes place and the converts are integrated into the full life of the church. In this way the external organization of the church year orders the internal experience of repentance, conversion, instruction, and incorporation into the life of the church. This cycle involves not only the converting persons, but the whole congregation in a process of renewal.

Second, implementation of liturgical evangelism requires local adaptability. In this book I have attempted to provide the full gamut of ceremonies, symbols, traditions, and rituals from both the ancient practice of liturgical evangelism and from the newer customs of liturgical evangelism. For most Protestant churches, the full use of these symbols is several levels away from their present practice. Therefore, keep in mind the major principle of change and growth: a person or group has difficulty understanding a language two levels or more away from their present experience. Growth in understanding best occurs when a person or congregation is stretched only one level beyond their present experience.

For example, a young Protestant man dating a girl from a Greek Orthodox tradition recently came to me asking for an explanation of the difference between orthodoxy and Protestant evangelical thought. I gave him what I thought was a perfectly clear explanation. Several weeks later I saw him and asked him how things were coming along in his attempt to understand Greek orthodoxy. He responded, "Thanks for your comments . . . I recently talked to a fellow student who grew up in the Greek Orthodox tradition and she really helped me understand it." Because my understanding of Greek orthodoxy is theological and academic and the fellow student's grasp was practical and experimental, she was able to speak a language that communicated more readily to the inquiring student. This same principle applies to the adaptation of evangelism through worship in the local church. A person or congregation must be stretched no more than one level at a time.

This principle will apply to the rites of liturgical evangelism in particular. For example, most liturgical churches such as the Episcopal and Lutheran churches may be able to use these rituals readily. However, churches such as Presbyterian, Methodist, or United Church of Christ will require greater adaptation. Other churches, such as Baptist and free church denominations, will require even more adaptation to get closer to the tolerance level of their congregation.

For those congregations that decide to implement liturgical evangelism, I suggest studying the *Rite of Christian Initiation of Adults* and the *RCIA: The Rites Revisited* by Sandra De Gidio. The first of these books will provide the recommended text of each rite. The second will illustrate how these rites have been adapted to different congregations. These two sources will help a congregation make intelligent adaptations.

The churches that have experimented with evangelism through worship have experienced an overwhelming sense of renewal throughout the entire church. Because the purpose of this book has been limited to an introduction to liturgical evangelism, I have not attempted to detail the experiences of particular churches. However, for those who want a practical pastoral account, I recommend Raymond B. Kemp's *A Journey in Faith,* which details the experience of a local congregation.

The reappearance of liturgical evangelism in the twentieth century may be hailed as one of the most significant developments in evangelism in this century. It not only represents the cutting edge of local church evangelism, but also promises to foster renewal on every level of congregational life. The time has come for the fire that has begun in the Catholic church to spread to the Protestant faith.

Bibliography

Austin, Gerard. *The Rite of Confirmation: Anointing with the Spirit.* New York: Pueblo, 1985.

Ball, Peter. *Adult Believing: A Guide to the Christian Initiation of Adults.* New York: Paulist Press, 1985.

Bourgeois, Henri. *On Becoming Christian: Christian Initiation and its Sacraments.* Mystic, CT: Twenty Third Publications, 1984.

Boyalk, Kenneth. *Catholic Evangelization Today: A New Pentecost for the United States.* New York: Paulist Press, 1985.

Christian Initiation Resources Reader. vol I Precatechumenate; vol. II Catechumenate; vol. III Purification and Enlightenment; vol. IV Mystagogia and Ministries. New York: Sadlier, 1984.

Conn, Walter E. *Conversion: Perspectives on Personal and Social Transformation.* New York: Abba House, 1978.

DeGidio, Sandra, O.S.M. *RCIA: The Rites Revisited.* Minneapolis, MN: Winston Press, 1984.

Dix, Gregory and Henry Chadwick, eds. *The Treatise on the Apostolic Tradition of St. Hippolytus of Rome.* Harrisburg, PA: Morehouse Publishing, 1992.

Duffy, Regis A., O.F.M. *On Becoming a Catholic: The Challenge of Christian Initiation.* San Francisco: Harper & Row, 1984.

Duggan, Robert, ed. *Conversion and the Catechumenate.* New York: Paulist Press, 1984.

Dujarier, Michel. *A History of the Catechumenate: The First Six Centuries.* New York: Sadlier, 1979.

_____. *The Rites of Christian Initiation: Historical and Pastoral Reflection,* Kevin Hart, trans. and ed. New York: Sadlier, 1979.

Dunning, James B. *New Wine: New Wineskins.* New York: Sadlier, 1981.

Eastman, A. Theodore. *The Baptizing Community: Christian Initiation and the Local Congregation.* Harrisburg, PA: Morehouse Publishing, 1991.

Easton, Burton Scott. *The Apostolic Tradition of Hippolytus.* Hamden, CT: Archon Books, 1962.

Eliade, Mircea. *Rites and Symbols of Initiation: The Mysteries of Birth and Rebirth.* New York: Harper & Brothers, 1958.

Ellebracht, Mary Pierre. *The Easter Passage: The RCIA Experience.* New York: Winston Press, 1983.

Green, Michael. *Evangelism in the Early Church.* Grand Rapids, MI: Eerdmans, 1970.

Hamma, Robert M. ed. *A Catechumen's Lectionary.* New York: Paulist Press, 1988.

Hinson, Glenn E. *The Evangelization of the Roman Empire.* Macon, GA: Mercer University Press, 1981.

Holash, Lise M. *Evangelization, The Catechumenate and its Ministries.* Dubuque, IA: Wm. C. Brown Company Publishers, 1983.

Huck, Gabe. *The Three Days: Parish Prayer in the Paschal Tradition.* Chicago: Liturgy Training Publications, 1981.

Johnson, Lawrence, ed. *Initiation and Conversion.* Collegeville, MN: The Liturgical Press, 1985.

Kavanaugh, Aidan. *Elements of Rite.* New York: Pueblo, 1966.

_____. *The Shape of Baptism: The Rite of Christian Initiation.* New York: Pueblo, 1978.

Kemp, Raymond B. *A Journey in Faith: An Experience of the Catechumenate.* New York: Sadlier, 1979.

MacMullen, Ramsay. *Christianizing the Roman Empire (A.D. 100-400).* New Haven, CT: Yale University Press, 1984.

Made, Not Born: New Perspectives on Christian Initiation and the Catechumenate. The Murphy Center for Liturgical Research. Notre Dame: University of Notre Dame Press, 1976.

Mazza, Enrico. *Mystagogy: A Theology of Liturgy in the Patristic Age.* New York: Pueblo, 1989.

Mick, Larry. *RCIA: Renewing the Church as an Initiating Assembly.* Collegeville, MN: The Liturgical Press, 1989.

Mitchell, Leonel L. *The Meaning of Ritual.* Harrisburg, PA: Morehouse Publishing, 1987.

Neville, Gwen Kennedy and John H. Westerhoff, III. *Learning Through Liturgy.* New York: Seabury, 1978.

Osborne, Kenan B. *The Christian Sacraments of Initiation: Baptism, Confirmation, Eucharist.* New York: Paulist Press, 1978.

Ostidiek, Gilbert. *Catechesis for Liturgy.* Washington, DC: The Pastoral Press, 1986.

Rath, Christine. *A Lay Person's Guide to the RCIA.* Dubuque, IA: Brown Publishing, 1989.

Reedy, J. William, ed. *Becoming a Catholic Christian: A Symposium on Christian Initiation.* New York: Sadlier, 1981.

Rite of Christian Initiation of Adults. Study Edition. Chicago: Liturgy Training Publication, 1988.

Searle, Mark. *Christening: The Making of Christians.* Collegeville: The Liturgical Press, 1980.

Shaughnessy, James D. *The Roots of Ritual.* Grand Rapids, MI: Eerdmans, 1973.

Smith, Gregory Michael. *The Fire in Their Eyes: Spiritual Mentors for the Christian Life.* New York: Paulist Press, 1984.

Stenick, Daniel B. *Baptismal Moments, Baptismal Meaning.* New York: The Church Hymnal Corporation, 1987.

Stokes, Kenneth. *Faith is a Verb: Dynamics of Adult Faith Development.* Mystic, CT: Twenty Third Publications, 1989.

Wagner, Johannes, ed. *Adult Baptism and the Catechumenate.* Concilium U. 22. New York: Paulist Press, 1967.

Wilde, James, ed. *Rite of Christian Initiation of Adults.* Chicago: Liturgy Training Publications, 1988.

Willimon, William. *Remembering Who You Are: Baptism, a Model for Christian Life.* Nashville: The Upper Room, 1980.

Yarnold, Edward, S.J., ed. *The Awe-Inspiring Rites of Initiation: Baptismal Homilies of the Fourth Century.* London, England: St. Paul Publications, 1981.

Index